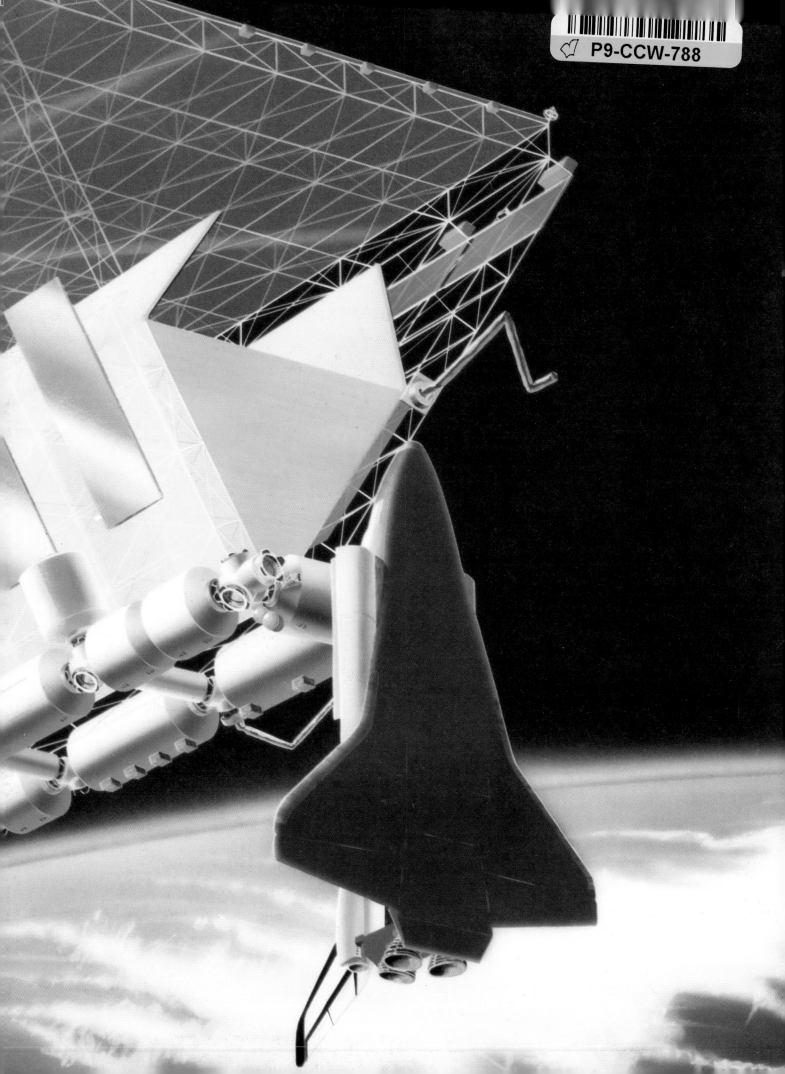

WAR IN SPACE

NIGEL FLYNN

Exeter Books

NEW YORK

"Defense at the speed

Designer: Chris Walker
Production: Richard Churchill

First published in USA 1986
by Exeter Books
Distributed by Bookthrift
Exeter is a trademark of Bookthrift Marketing, Inc.
Bookthrift is a registered trademark of Bookthrift Marketing
New York, New York

ISBN 0–671–08212–4
© Marshall Cavendish Limited 1986

Printed and bound in Spain by Jerez Industrial, S.A.

"...f light"

CONTENTS

FOREWORD

PROLOGUE
'A VISION OF THE FUTURE'
6

CHAPTER 1
'THE ULTIMATE HIGH GROUND'
10

CHAPTER 2
'THE BOLT FROM OUT OF THE BLUE'
22

CHAPTER 3
'THE MAGINOT LINE OF THE 21st CENTURY'
38

CHAPTER 4
'TAKING THE TWINKLE OUT OF STARLIGHT'
56

CHAPTER 5
'OUT THERE WHERE THE PEOPLE AREN'T'
86

GLOSSARY

FURTHER READING

INDEX

FOREWORD

When President Reagan made his 'Star Wars' speech in March 1983, describing the day when impenetrable hi-tech defences would render nuclear-tipped ICBMs obsolete, it took everyone by surprise. Since then, the so-called Strategic Defense Initiative (SDI) has hardly been out of the headlines – but few people really understand what it is about. This book provides an admirable analysis of military space activities in general and Star Wars in particular – today's research and what it could look like in operation around the turn of the century.

There has been a strong military interest in space since the 84 kg Soviet Sputnik 1, emitting a plaintive beep-beep as it circled the globe once every 96 minutes, signalled the dawn of the Space Age. Whole fleets of spy satellites from both the US and USSR now maintain a constant watch on military installations and movements, listen to radio transmissions and scan for rocket launches. Both sides play down their military space programmes – the Soviet Union barely acknowledges its existence – but the reality is that around three-quarters of the world's space launches each year have military missions and most are hidden by the Soviet 'Cosmos' catch-all name. There were 121 space launches in 1985, of which 98 originated from the three USSR sites at Plesetsk, Tyuratam and Kapustin Yar. The US accounted for only 17, the European Space Agency for three, and Japan and China for two and one each, respectively.

The Soviet Union has had a large lead in numbers since the early 1970s but it can be a misleading statistic. Most American military satellites carry out their duties for months or even years while their Soviet counterparts quite often survive for only a few weeks. The military programmes are evenly matched in results, although the Shuttle tragedy has severely disrupted the West's launch schedule – the new sophisticated KH-12 photo-reconnaissance satellite will be delayed, for example. Both sides also suffer unmanned failures. The US lost a KH-11 spysat in a $150 million launch failure during August 1985 and the Soviets saw one of their radio eavesdroppers stranded in the wrong orbit the following December.

While the Americans are having to work hard to recover from the Shuttle loss in January 1986, the whole Soviet programme is stepping into a higher gear. Three new space

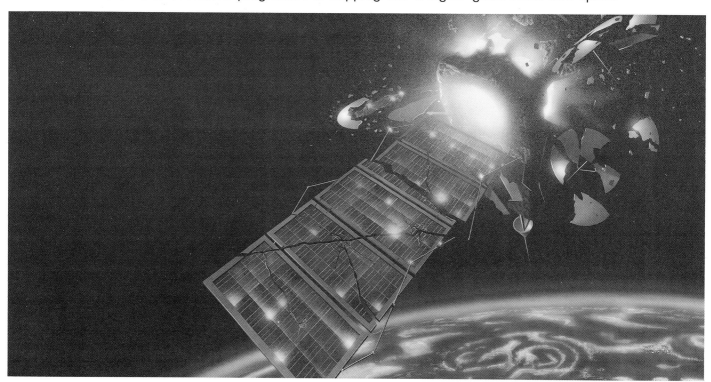

launchers are expected soon, two carrying small- and large-winged shuttles with crews aboard. The new Mir space station is forming the basis of a permanently manned orbital complex at a time when the US station is not expected to be operational until the mid-1990s. The Soviets are also planning an exciting series of sophisticated robot probes to the Moon, Mars, comets and asteroids as American scientists stand back in admiration. On this occasion, the frequently expressed fear that the West is dropping behind could well be appropriate. There is even the suggestion that a manned Mars mission will be easily within reach by 1995 — less than a decade away.

It is against this background that the SDI research programme is being conducted. Work on space lasers, particle beams and kinetic energy weapons has been under way for years but what President Reagan did was tie the strands together into a single plan that we now call Star Wars. Whether it will work at all is too difficult a question to answer at this early stage. The idea is often criticised on two fronts. Firstly, it will be so incredibly complicated that it could never work as a whole, the critics say, even if the individual parts are technically feasible. It would have to work so rapidly and accurately that it would have to be under computer control, and some scientists claim it will be impossible to perfect the tens of millions of lines of computer programs. Even its supporters do not pretend that it could provide 100 per cent protection against incoming warheads — a number will always get through.

The second criticism is more philosophical. For several decades now, both sides have had sufficient long-range weapons to ensure that neither could survive a full-scale conflict. There is no point in one side launching a surprise attack because it would still suffer punishing losses in the inevitable response. The Mutually Assured Destruction (MAD) doctrine clearly works to some extent because we are still here. Star Wars could tear apart the whole shaky system and whoever perfected it first would surely be tempted to launch a preemptive strike safe in the knowledge that their defences would stop any retaliation.

Of course, the present studies could prove the whole system would be just too expensive. It is no good building up a perfect network of defences if the other side can then make a relatively cheap alteration in its method of attack. That way, it would be a constantly changing entity sucking in a never-ending stream of money. Could it even be tested except in an actual war? To test the X-ray laser pop-up system in space, for example, would be in direct contravention of the 1963 Partial Test Ban Treaty.

The military satellites whirling around over our heads at the moment are largely passive, quietly observing what is going on below but taking no active part in it. That could change with SDI. The next century could well see weapons being raised off the two-dimensional surface of planet Earth and into the third dimension of space as a result of today's studies. It is a story that should engage everyone's attention.

Andrew Wilson
Space Coordinator
Space Information Bureau
Managing Editor, British Interplanetary Society 1981–85

Left: *A kinetic energy weapon destroys its target — here an 'enemy' military satellite — by the impact of the collision. Star Wars systems will end the relative sanctity that satellites have hitherto enjoyed in space.*

PROLOGUE: 'A VISION OF THE FUTURE'

President Ronald Reagan, March 23, 1983

IN WASHINGTON DC that night, no one, not even the President's closest advisors, knew exactly what he would say when he made his scheduled speech to the nation. Only minutes before stepping out in front of the television cameras, Defense Secretary Caspar Weinberger telephoned the White House in a final attempt to stop the speech. But as the world was soon to learn, the attempt failed.

Two thousand miles away, on the other side of the dark continent, computer consoles in the Space Defense Operations Center flickered their tiny lights of warning as the space frontier is scanned for the first signs of a war no one wants.

With the easy charm of the professional actor, Ronald Wilson Reagan,

72-year-old President of the United States, clears his throat and smiles. "Let me share a vision of the future that offers hope," he invites his audience. "It is that we embark on a programme to counter the awesome Soviet missile threat with measures that are defensive." With the aid of charts, diagrams and statistics, the President chronicles the massive missile build-up. There is a pause, perfectly timed, before he continues.

"What if free people could live secure in the knowledge that their security did not rest upon the threat of instant US retaliation to deter a Soviet attack; that we could intercept and destroy strategic ballistic missiles before they reached our soil or that of our allies? . . . Would it not be better to save lives than to avenge them?

"I call upon the scientific community who gave us nuclear weapons to turn their great talents to the cause of mankind and world peace: to give us the means of rendering these nuclear missiles impotent and obsolete.

"My fellow Americans, tonight we are launching an effort which holds the promise of changing the course of human history. There will be risks, and results take time. But with your support, I believe we can do it."

Reaction to the President's speech was swift, though uncertain. In the Pentagon, the next day, America's top brass were seen rushing round asking "what the hell is 'strategic defence?'" Members of the Reagan Administration were no better placed to answer. Secretary of State, General Alexander Haig, was later to give his view of how the speech came to be made. "The White House guys said, 'Hey, boss, come on. You're going to make a big splash. Big PR. You're going to look like the greatest leader in America. Get out there and give that speech.' And he did."

In London, *The Times* quoted a US 'defence specialist' as saying that the President's proposals were "terrifying", "unworkable", and "bizarre". In Moscow, ageing Soviet leader, Yuri Andropov, reacted strongly against the US "bid to disarm the Soviet Union". And, to ensure that the White House got the message, added that the USSR "would never be caught defenceless".

Senator Edward Kennedy set the tone of the debate when he called the speech a hotch-potch of "misleading scare tactics and reckless Star Wars schemes". The jibe stuck, and despite later insistence that the President's programme be called by its official label, "Strategic Defence Initiative" (SDI), it soon became known, almost universally as "Star Wars".

But it was not just the name that perplexed commentators the morning after. What they wanted to know was, if the Pentagon and the State Department knew so little about the speech, who *was* behind it, and could such a space-based, anti-ballistic missile (ABM) system *really* work?

The story of the men and the ideas that shaped the President's speech — a speech that was to mark the most significant shift in US strategic thinking for a quarter of a century — revolves around the personality of the President himself, and his close association with a nuclear physicist, a retired army general and the deputy director of America's top secret organization, the Defense Intelligence Agency.

In 1967, Ronald Reagan, then Governor of California, visited the Lawrence Livermore National Laboratory in Livermore, California. Founded in the 1950s by Dr Edward ('father of the H-bomb') Teller, the Laboratory was then, and is now, a secret government weapons establishment and the centre for advanced laser fusion research. The Governor's visit marked the beginning of an association between the two men that was to have important repercussions for America's strategic planning when Ronald Reagan entered the White House.

Above: *Star Wars architect, President Reagan.*
Left: *An orbiting laser battle cruiser about to intercept an ICBM (shown by the orange and white flash).*

The research that Dr Teller was personally engaged in was the nuclear X-ray laser — a futuristic device (code-named 'Excalibur') first tested beneath the Nevada desert on November 14, 1980, under the official code-name 'Dauphin'. In theory, the weapon is simple enough. It consists of an orbiting nuclear bomb which, when detonated, releases multiple laser beams. Directed at incoming Soviet ICBMs it would destroy everything in its path before it was itself consumed in a nuclear fire-ball. This device, Dr Teller believed, would provide the United States with the defence against nuclear missiles he had always claimed was possible, despite the fact that the use of such a weapon in space is banned by treaty. But, as we shall see in Chapter 4, the X-ray laser was to play an important part in the formulation of the 'Star Wars' strategy.

In May 1981 President Reagan appointed Dr George A. Keyworth II as his personal scientific advisor. The appointment was made with the approval of Dr Teller. George Keyworth — who was to be almost unique among the President's men in being consulted on the Star Wars speech — was a nuclear physicist, well versed in the X-ray laser secrets. It was a weapon in which he took a personal interest. Speaking at the Lawrence Livermore Laboratory on January 14, 1983 (two months before the President made his speech), Dr Keyworth was the first government official to admit the existence of the device when he praised the assembled scientists for their work on the "bomb-pumped X-ray laser", and stated that it was "one of the most important programmes that may seriously influence the nation's defense posture in the next decades."

That the newly elected President was predisposed to look favourably on the advice of those advocating space-based ABM defence, is well illustrated by a visit he made a few months before his election in 1980, to the North American Aerospace Defense Command (NORAD) centre located deep inside the hollowed-out Cheyenne Mountain in Colorado. Later, the President was to recall his sense of wonderment when he realized that here, "they actually are tracking several thousand objects in space, meaning satellites of ours and everyone else's, even down to the point that they are tracking a glove lost by an astronaut." But, he continued, "I think the thing that struck me was the irony that here, with this great technology of ours, we can do all this, yet we cannot stop any of the weapons that are coming at us. I don't think there's been a time in history when there wasn't a defense against some kind of thrust, even back in the old-fashioned days when we had coast artillery that would stop invading ships."

Slowly, the idea of a space-based strategic policy began to take shape in the President's mind. It was assisted in 1981 by the formation of a group of top scientists, industrialists and military men under the directorship of Karl R. Bendetson, former Under Secretary of the Army, and a leading member of the influential Hoover Institution on War, Revolution and Peace.

Calling themselves the Heritage Foundation, the group set up business in Washington DC with generous funding from a number of undisclosed, private sources. The group's deputy director was an ex-Army Lt. General, Daniel O. Graham, who had also served as director of the Defense Intelligence Agency and advisor to Ronald Reagan in the 1976 and 1980 campaigns. The aim of the group was to publicize the growing danger of Soviet nuclear aggression, and bring public pressure to bear upon the White House to increase America's defence spending in order to reassert American nuclear superiority. The group included Dr Edward Teller, and it was not long before the Heritage Foundation was advocating that the United States abandon the concept of 'Mutual Assured Destruction' (known by the appropriate acronym MAD), which had guided America's strategic nuclear thinking since the 1960s, in favour of a 'defensive' policy consisting of a laser battle fleet, based in space. But divisions

within the group, which centred upon the speed with which such a system could and should be deployed, led to the creation of a splinter group.

Taking with him those members of the group who believed that the United States had within its power the ability to deploy such a system within a matter of years, General Graham created an organization called 'High Frontier Incorporated'. By 1982 they were ready to report their findings to the President. Dismissed by the Pentagon as the work of a bunch of cranks, the report nevertheless made a deep impression upon the President.

Under the title *We Must Defend America,* 'Project Director' Daniel O. Graham, lists (in the 1983 edition) the following formula to solve "not only our security problems, but also economic, political, and moral issues facing the nation. If adopted, High Frontier would accomplish the following:

- Replace the failed and morally suspect doctrine of Mutual Assured Destruction (MAD) with a strategy of Assured Survival;
- Create a reliable effective deterrent to nuclear war by defending the United States and the Free World rather than by threatening a suicidal punitive strike at Soviet civilians;
- Create an immediate surge in the high-technology sector of the US economy by opening and securing space for private enterprise;
- Provide positive and challenging goals for American youth and a restored image of US success and leadership abroad;
- Do all the above at costs to the taxpayer below all other available alternatives to meet the current Soviet threat;
- And do so with or without Soviet co-operation."

As Lt. General Graham explains in his first chapter, such a programme of national resurgence is necessary to combat "the stench of appeasement, pacifism, self-flagellation and abandonment of principle [that] hangs heavy over our land." The book was dedicated to Ronald Reagan, was endorsed by the President in a letter to Graham of June 3, in which he said that the book had "rendered . . . an in-

valuable service for which all future generations will be grateful".

But in January 1983, there were still a number of events and a series of meetings before the President finally committed himself, and the nation, to 'strategic defence'. On February 11, in the midst of the biggest snow storm Washington had seen in four years, the President met the Joint Chiefs of Staff. Top of the agenda was the deployment of the new MX ("some of my best friends" – Ronald Reagan) missiles. It was a subject that was complicated and fraught with political difficulties. The President, bored,

and convince Congress of the need to increase defence spending. John Hughes, deputy director for Intelligence and External Affairs at the Defense Intelligence Agency, and the man who had briefed John F. Kennedy throughout the Cuban missile crisis, had been enlisted to sell the controversial budget to a suspicious Congress and public. In a series of slide shows at the White House, Hughes demonstrated with the aid of spy satellite pictures, the Soviet missile build-up and secret Russian installations in Cuba, Grenada and Nicaragua. According to Republican Senator Stevens of Alaska, no normal person could have listened to Hughes' briefing and not come out without his hair standing on end. Nevertheless, Hughes failed, and the President's budget was rejected on March 23, 1983 – the very day he was scheduled to make his long awaited speech to the nation.

Nor was the President oblivious to the growing support shown for Senator Edward Kennedy's nuclear freeze movement: even the staunchly Reaganite state of California had voted in a referendum in favour of the freeze. It was time, the President realized, to say something to stem the tide of political dissent. To White House aides, what was needed was a 'speech insert' or 'coda' that would make the massive $1,600,000 million five-year military budget more palatable to the public. Assisted by George Keyworth and Robert 'Bud' McFarlane, deputy National Security Advisor, the President wrote his secret 'coda'.

No details were given by the President about the sort of ABM system he was considering. Official spokesmen, interviewed later that night, mentioned, vaguely, satellites, lasers, particle beam weapons, and other "high tech items", but again, no details were given. They were careful, too, to stress that the President's proposals consisted of a research and development programme only. There was no question, for the present at least, of such a system being deployed, even if the technology was available. And it was doubtful whether a full space-based ABM system would be operational until the beginning of the 21st century.

From the comments of officials that night, no one would have known that the war in space had begun.

began to doodle the outline of a horse's head and a cowboy on the pad in front of him. But, according to one participant, at the mention of "strategic defense" as a possible policy option, the President's eyes focused and he kept the discussion flowing for half an hour – far longer than those involved thought the subject warranted. Nevertheless, when the President asked, rhetorically, "would it not be better to defend lives than to avenge them?", those who knew him well realized that it signalled a major policy change.

The scene was now set for the

Above: *The launching of an MX 'Peacemaker' ICBM. The problem of how to protect the MX led directly to Star Wars research.*

public unveiling of the President's 'Strategic Defense Initiative'. And when the House of Representatives voted decisively, by 229 votes to 196, in favour of a Democrat budget proposal which cut deep into defence spending, White House aides knew the time had come for the President to 'make a big splash'.

Every pressure had been used to try

CHAPTER 1

'THE ULTIMATE HIGH GROUND'

'Space is the ultimate high ground'
Aerospace: Basic Doctrine, USAF Manual

"Talk about the dangers of extending the arms race to
space is a bit of a myth. What is not generally
appreciated is the extent and the speed
with which outer space has been put
to military use."

Bhupendra Jasani, International Peace Research Institute, Stockholm

JUST OFF LOCKHEED WAY, in Sunnyvale, northern California, lies the US Space Division's Satellite Control Facility. There are no windows in the nine-storey, pale-blue building, known as the 'Big Blue Cube', for prying eyes to see in. A large notice displayed at the gate warns visitors:

IDENTIFICATION REQUIRED BEYOND THIS POINT. USE OF DEADLY FORCE AUTHORIZED.

'Beyond this point' lies the Satellite Test Center, nerve centre of the worldwide network of US Remote Tracking Stations. There are seven other satellite tracking centres, flung around the globe – the Seychelles; United States Air Force Base Guam, South Pacific; Oahu, Hawaii; Thule, Greenland; Oakhanger, England (south west of London off the A3); Manchester, New Hampshire; and US Air Force Base Vandenberg, California.

Each station is linked to Sunnyvale, and each station, or 'facility', has a complex of computers and communications to track and receive telemetry (transmitted data) from US orbiting military satellites, deep in space. Data beamed down is transmitted from each station to the Big Blue Cube, where it is 'processed' and forwarded to key US military command posts, worldwide.

At the push of a button, ground controllers can direct their satellites at will. By activating the satellite's small booster rockets, they can change or maintain the satellite's orbital flight-path, switch its cameras on or off, instruct it to radio down information it has gathered, or report on its own condition.

In addition to Space Division's tracking stations, the newly formed USAF Space Command maintains a global Space Detection and Tracking System (SPADATS), which tracks and records the progress of all 5,500 man-made satellites and space debris orbiting the Earth. The tracking stations of SPADATS, which includes the US Navy's Space Surveillance System, Canada's Satellite Tracking Unit and the USAF system, ('Spacetracks'), feed information to the headquarters of NORAD, the North American Aerospace Defense Command, located beneath the

Above: *The USAF Satellite Control Facility ('Big Blue Cube'), Sunnyvale, California.*
Left: *US astronaut takes a space walk.*

hollowed-out granite Cheyenne Mountain. Here, where the first signs of the final war will be seen, is also housed the Space Defense Operations Center. Its job will be to orchestrate the anti-satellite battles of the future.

These Air Force facilities are planned to be supplemented by the new multi-million dollar Consolidated Space Operations Center (CSOC) under construction nine miles east of Peterson Air Force Base, near Colorado Springs, Colorado. Scheduled to open in December 1987, having suffered numerous delays, the Center will accommodate the USAF Space Command and will control future space shuttle missions, in addition to providing satellite tracking and control facilities.

Alongside the USAF ground tracking stations, keeping their watchful eye on US military assets in space, are the secret, ground tracking stations of the CIA (Central Intelligence Agency). Exactly how many spy satellites are maintained by the CIA is in itself an official secret. But information from ex-CIA agents suggests that the Agency's photographic and electronic intelligence gathering satellites are monitored by a worldwide network of stations; one of which is located near Alice Springs in Australia from where raw data is fed to a clandestine CIA station buried within the TRW Defense and Space Systems Group at Redondo Beach, California. From these two installations, and possibly many others, reports are filed to the CIA Operations Center at Langley in Virginia.

To wage war on Earth, the two superpowers are now dependent on space. In any future conflict, the first moves made by an aggressor will be to eliminate the enemy's space-

Above: *Forerunner of the Space Shuttle Dyna-Soar was to be launched into orbit by the Titan rocket and glide back to Earth.*

based intelligence, communications, control and command facilities. "Even in a limited war," admits George A. Keyworth, President Reagan's top scientific advisor, "we would have an absolutely critical dependence on space today. Survivability of our space assets is one of our most important priorities." The war that everyone hopes will never be fought on Earth, is being waged, silently in outer space, day by day.

The idea of placing an artificial satellite in space to spy on an enemy's activities was first discussed by the Pentagon in 1946. But it was not until the development of the giant rockets capable of lobbing a nuclear warhead across continents, in the mid-1950s, that the means to place a satellite in space became available.

On October 4, 1957, the world awoke to the news that Sputnik 1, the world's first man-made satellite had been successfully launched by the Soviet Union. In the United States, members of the Eisenhower Administration returned to their desks that day in a state of shock. It seemed incredible that the Soviet Union, a supposedly backward peasant society, should possess the technology to perform such a feat. Understandably, the Pentagon was stunned.

Eisenhower, however, seemed unimpressed. A "little ball in the sky" is what he called it until he was told that Soviet spy satellites could threaten national security. With the launch of America's first satellite, Explorer 1, on February 1, 1958, the race in space was on. Though the reality of space-flight in those early days seems primitive by today's standards,

it was, at the time, felt that the space age had dawned.

In the United States, opinion was divided on the question of how the space programme should be administered, and in what direction it should develop. The Army claimed its share of whatever research and development money there was, since it had been their Ballistic Missile Agency, headed by German-born Wernhier von Braun (the man who had invented the V-2 rocket that had been hurled against Britain in the final months of World War II), that had provided the Jupiter-C launch vehicle for Explorer 1. They also had elaborate plans for a fleet of rocket transporters to ferry men and equipment across continents, and a blueprint for the establishment of Army installations on the Moon.

Jealous of the Army's role, the Air Force had its own plans and space research team. In November 1957, just a month after Sputnik 1 had taken its place in Earth orbit, the Air Force issued a directive for the development of a super space plane called Dyna-Soar — a name derived from the craft's most notable characteristics, "dynamic" and "soaring". Like the space shuttle, which was to appear 20 years later, Dyna-Soar was designed to fly through space at hypersonic speed and glide back to Earth in the manner of a conventional aircraft.

Though millions of dollars were poured into the project it was scrapped in 1963 when the concept of a space-glider was dropped in favour of the more expensive, but potentially more prestigious, Apollo Moon programme.

In 1958, however, these events were still a long way off. That autumn, President Eisenhower resisted demands to militarize space and created instead the civilian controlled National Aeronautics and Space Administration (NASA). NASA was to be a model for the international exchange of scientific information and co-operation, pledged to the peaceful exploration of space. There were others, however, who had other ideas for the new satellites then orbiting the globe.

A month after the launching of Explorer I, the first US spy satellite (officially designated a reconnaissance satellite or 'reconsat') Discoverer I lifted off on top of a Thor-

Agena rocket from Vandenberg Air Force Base, California. Though the launch and all subsequent twelve Discovery launches ended in failure, the Air Force was firmly committed to the idea of satellite spying. But the Pentagon and the Department of Defense had still to be fully convinced. On May 1, 1960, the military spacemen were given their chance.

On that day a solitary U-2 spy plane, piloted by CIA agent, Francis Gary Powers, was shot down by a Soviet surface-to-air (SAM) missile while on a photo-reconnaissance mission near the rocket launch site at Sverdlovsk, 31 miles (50km) south west of Tyuratum. Without their U-2 high-flying spy planes, the Pentagon was temporarily "blinded". Clearly, other means had to be found.

Three months after the U-2 incident, on August 10, 1960, Discoverer 13 rose above the Californian coast and reached Earth-orbit. Within a year the Pentagon was regularly receiving film returned to Earth by space capsule, showing secret Soviet military installations. Nor were the Russians far behind. In 1962 Cosmos 4, the first Soviet spy satellite was launched. Both sides knew what the other was doing, but a strange unspoken agreement arose between them not to say anything, publicly at least,

about the other side's spying activities.

And in many ways the development of space spy satellites has helped to keep the peace. The number, deployment and range of each other's nuclear forces could be clearly seen. The nuclear test ban treaties could be properly monitored, and thanks to the early warning (EW) satellites, neither side could launch a surprise nuclear attack against the other without it being detected. The knowledge that such an attack had been launched would itself guarantee immediate retaliation from the other side. Thus the concept of Mutual Assured Destruction (MAD) was born.

Today, each side jealously guards its satellite secrets. The numbers launched, their role and performance, are some of the world's most closely guarded secrets. In the USSR there has been a blanket silence on the subject since the early 1960s. Soviet spy satellites carry no special designation and are part of the all-embracing Cosmos space programme. In the USA, the Kennedy Administration imposed a total ban on the publication of details relating to spy satellites in 1961 on the insistence of the CIA. Not until 1978, when President Jimmy Carter referred to their use for the first time in public, was their existence admitted.

Above: *In July 1984 this picture, taken by US spy satellite KH-11, showing the Soviet nuclear-powered aircraft-carrier Kremlin, was leaked to a magazine by US Navy analyst Samuel Morrison, later convicted for doing so.*

What little is known about the number of launches, range and performance of spy satellites has been painstakingly assembled by defence analysts working with knowledge of a basic physics, assumptions about current satellite technology, press leaks, and the evidence brought to light by two major spy trials held in the United States in the late 1970s.

On January 16, 1977, a twenty-two year-old College drop-out, Christopher John Boyce was arrested by FBI agents on the charge of spying for the Soviet Union. At his trial, Boyce revealed that he had been hired by the CIA to process classified information received from the CIA's secret satellite, code-named 'Rhyolite'. Data from the satellite was sent either via the CIA outpost near Alice Springs, Australia, or direct to Boyce in the 'Black Vault' – a secret installation run by the CIA and located within the giant TRW defence complex at Redondo Beach, California. From there·the information was sent, as far as Boyce knew, to the CIA Operations Center, Langley, Virginia; though some maintain, however, that a more likely destination was Fort Meade, Maryland, home of the National Security Agency which specializes in ELINT (electronic intelligence) operations. Most of the information that flowed through Boyce's hands related to the Soviet Union and China. But some, to Boyce's surprise and horror, concerned the internal affairs of friendly, allied governments, such as Australia. This upset Boyce the idealist and, determined to get his own back on an organization that he had come to despise, he decided to sell his secrets to the Russians.

The CIA 'Rhyolite' satellite, still in service under a new code-name, is an electronic intelligence (ELINT) gathering satellite, known in the trade as a 'ferret'. Ferrets are used to monitor 'enemy' radar, radio and telephone traffic, and relay the messages back when the craft passes over its own ground tracking stations. Rhyolite satellites bristle with electronic surveillance equipment and take a particular interest in the traffic of communications emanating from the Soviet ICBM test and satellite launch centre at Tyuratum. The giant 70ft (21.3m) dish antenna that adorns the satellite, is reputed to be able to pick up telephone conversations of Russian soldiers stationed at the base.

The first Rhyolite was launched on March 6, 1973, and took up sentry duty 22,300 miles (35,880km) above the Horn of Africa, in the Indian Ocean. At this distance from Earth a satellite appears to an observer on the ground to be stationary – hence the term 'geostationary' or 'geosynchronous' orbit. In fact, of course, it only *appears* stationary because its velocity matches that of the Earth's, and also because it, too, takes 24 hours to complete its orbit. By 1983, another Rhyolite had joined the first, and a further pair positioned to track missile and satellite launches from the Soviet base at Plesetsk, in central USSR.

From within the 'Black Vault', Boyce passed secret information to his friend Andrew Daulton Lee, a professional drug-pusher with a lengthy criminal record. Lee in turn sold the secrets to the Soviet Embassy in New

Above: *One of the few pictures of a spy satellite being launched – the sophisticated Big Bird on top of the Titan 3D/Agena.*

Mexico. For two years the flow of information, some valuable, some worthless, continued until the FBI finally caught up with them.

At the same time as Boyce was passing secrets of the Rhyolite system to the Russians, the CIA was testing a new, revolutionary, type of photo-reconnaissance satellite. Called Key-Hole 11 (KH-11), it was not unlike the Big Bird spy satellite used by the Air Force. Both weighed some 14 tons, were between 40 to 50-ft long and 10-ft in diameter. KH-11, however, is one of the most sophisticated of US spy satellites currently in service. Nothing was known publicly of this satellite, not even its designation, until August 18, 1978, when two FBI agents arrested William P. Kampiles, the 23-year-old son of a Greek immigrant, for selling the top secret operating manual of KH-11 to the Russians. Like Boyce, Kampiles was a former agent of the CIA – based at the Operations Center, Langley, Virginia, where, although occupying a relatively lowly position, he nevertheless had access to secret documents – among them the KH-11 technical manual.

Placing copy numbered 155 in his coat pocket, Kampiles took the booklet home, because, he said, it looked "interesting". In October 1977 he was forced to resign from the

CIA or face dismissal for incompetence. After staying in his mother's flat for the winter, Kampiles journeyed to Athens in February 1978 to visit friends. On impulse, one day in March, he paid a visit to the Russian Embassy and, under a false name, offered to sell them his KH-11 manual, number 155. At first he handed over just a few pages to the Russian representative, Major Michael Zavali. Told that he would receive no money until he handed over the complete document, Kampiles complied, and in return received the princely sum of $3,000 (about £1,500).

Returning to the United States, Kampiles began work at a laboratory in Oak Brook, Illinois. Proud of his having been in the pay of both the CIA and the KGB, Kampiles could not resist boasting of his glamorous connections to a girl-friend. Unfortunately for Kampiles, the girl-friend also had close connections with secret service organizations, for on April 18, 1978, William Kampiles was picked up by the FBI. In December he was sentenced to 40 years imprisonment (the same sentence passed on

Christopher Boyce).

The Russians were naturally delighted to have secured such an important document so cheaply. Consequently, they now know more about the KH-11 than can be revealed in the West. However, defence analysts have been able to piece together a profile of the KH-11, which has not been officially contradicted or denied. Like Big Bird before it and the Rhyolite range of ferrets, KH-11 is launched by the giant Titan 34D rocket, the workhorse of the US space programme, though launching of the satellite from the space shuttle is scheduled for the near future. KH-11's polar flight path

takes it 310 miles (500km) away from Earth at its farthest point (known technically as the *apogee)*, and 155 miles (250km) as it swoops over the Soviet Union at its closest point to Earth (known as its *perigee*). Thus the KH-11, in common with most spy satellites, follows a markedly elliptical orbit (see diagram).

Unlike earlier photographic spy satellites, KH-11's cameras do not use film (which is bulky, has to be returned to Earth by capsule and shortens the duration of the satellite's flight). Instead, it uses a system of digital signal transmission. When the KH-11's telescopes scan the Earth, its light-sensitive electronic sensors translate these light patterns into digital signals. These signals are transmitted back to base where each signal is assigned one of several hundred tones, ranging from jet black to pure white, depending upon

the strength of the signal received. The 'picture' itself is made up of these varying tones. Though the image is not, perhaps, as sharp and as clear as the pictures taken by the more conventional TV cameras of Big Bird, the resolution achieved by KH-11 is nevertheless, impressive.

What can a spy satellite, 150 miles in space 'see'? This is usually answered in terms of 'ground resolution', that is, the size of the smallest object one can see in the picture. With the very best high-resolution film-return satellites (such as Big Bird), ground-resolution is said to be about six inches — which is enough to be able to read the headlines of a newspaper, or the number plates on a family car. A resolution of some 10 feet is sufficient to reveal missile launch sites; to identify the missiles themselves requires a resolution of some five feet; and to tell the particular type of missile, a ground resolution of two feet is adequate.

Fitted with multi-spectral scanning devices, the KH-11 can also take pictures at night and uncover camouflaged objects invisible to the naked eye. Military installations, airfields, rocket launch sites, submarine pens and missile bases are, of course, of prime interest. But in assessing Soviet power and potential, the CIA uses its surveillance satellites to gather information on Soviet agriculture, industrial plant, the location of mines, chemical industries and even, it is said, the square-footage available for the production of each category of military weapon.

In January 1984 the influential American magazine *Aviation Week & Space Technology* (a major source of 'official' leaks), stated that the production of two smaller Key-Hole satellites, KH-8 and KH-9, had stopped because of soaring costs and the need to re-direct the available resources to maintaining the enormously expensive KH-11. The existence of KH-9 had been revealed publicly for the first time in April 1983 when a press report described it as a "low-altitude-film-return spacecraft with a limited lifetime". According to the authoritative *Jane's Spaceflight Directory*, 1984, it was "used only to photograph highest-priority intelligence targets in the Soviet Union and elsewhere". What is not revealed by *Jane's* is that the mysterious satellite was probably involved in the Korean

Below: *The ill-fated space shuttle Challenger lifts-off on an earlier mission (STS-8) on the night of August 30, 1983.*

THE FATED FLIGHT OF KE 007

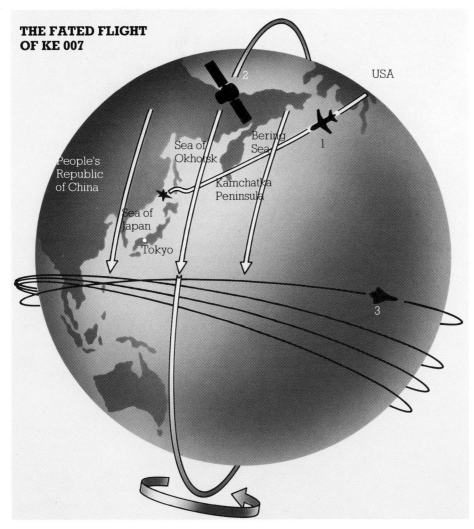

KAL KE 007 (1) *shot down over the Sea of Japan with the loss of 269 lives. Was it part of a spying operation involving 'ferret' 1982-41C* (2) *and STS-8* (3), *as some have claimed?*

Airline incident on the night of August 31/September 1, 1983.

When a Korean Airlines (KAL) Boeing 747 (though some reports state that it was a 707 – a difference that, as the story reveals, could be significant) was shot down by a Soviet SU-15 interceptor, killing 269 passengers, a report appeared in the Russian daily newspaper *Pravda* a few days later linking the incident to the presence of a US electronic intelligence spy satellite above the area where the aircraft was shot down. Though *Pravda* did not identify the satellite, evidence has since come to light that suggests that it was an ELINT satellite, designation number 1982-41C, launched from Vandenberg Air Force Base on May 11, 1982. The satellite, believed to be a KH-9,

rode 'piggyback' on the photo-reconnaissance satellite, Big Bird, but was then placed in independent orbit.

The ground track taken by the satellite at the time the Boeing 747 was over the Kamchatka Peninsula – one of the Soviet Union's most secret Anti-Ballistic Missile test sites – is shown above. Though the times at which the satellite passed over the region are the same as those reported by *Pravda*, the position of the ground tracks are different. The ground tracks in *Pravda* are shown to be closer together, suggesting that the satellite was travelling faster than is usual for an ELINT satellite of the type it is believed to have been. During the KAL incursion into Soviet airspace – once over Kamchatka, and again over the island of Sakhalin, 400 miles north of the aircraft's scheduled route – KH-9 crossed the area three times, as shown in the diagram.

The Soviet claim that the aircraft was involved in spying gains greater credibility by the revelation in the

New York Times on October 17, 1983, that a senior US Intelligence official had admitted that a US spy plane – a modified Boeing 707, called an RC-135 – *was* in the area on the night of the incident. According to the *Times* report, the official stated that electronic reconnaissance monitoring the conversations between the SU-15 pilot and Soviet ground control, showed conclusively that "the Soviet air defense command was operating on the assumption that the SU-15 was tracking a USAF RC-135 reconnaissance plane". The official also stated that the SU-15 was flying below the ill-fated Boeing rather than parallel to it, and that the pilot could easily have mistaken the aircraft's identity "given the difficulty of identifying a plane from below".

Further revelations by Dr Bhupendra Jasani, an expert on military activity in space at the Stockholm International Peace Research Institute (SIPRI), makes the whole incident even more curious. Writing in the SIPRI *Yearbook 1985,* Dr Jasani reports that the US space shuttle STS-8 Challenger was also in the area at roughly the same time as both the aircraft and the satellite (see diagram). Could the space shuttle, perhaps, have been operating as a command post, co-ordinating an intelligence operation involving both the satellite and the KAL Boeing 747, as some have claimed?

The truth of the incident will probably never be known, though the episode shows how big a part military satellites now play on the stage of international affairs.

On July 31, 1983, another KH-9 was launched from Vandenberg to spy on the new Soviet missile site at Abalakova, in central Siberia. This was the last launching, as far as is known, of KH-9's short, though undoubtedly active life. KH-8, its twin brother, appears to have spent its short life in total obscurity.

Right: *Military satellites follow certain orbits for chosen tasks. Soviet EW craft use* Highly Elliptical *orbits to maximize coverage of the Northern Hemisphere. US EW, ELINT and communications satellites follow a* Geosynchronous *orbit; 'close-look' spy satellites* Elliptical *orbits, and one in* Polar *orbit would in time survey the globe.*

SATELLITE ORBITS

HIGHLY ELLIPTICAL

POLAR

GEOSYNCHRONOUS

GEOSYNCHRONOUS

ELLIPTICAL

For centuries military theorists have taught that the occupation of the high ground (hills, ridges, anywhere that commands a vantage point), is essential for the prosecution of successful military operations. From the high ground you can see clearly every move the enemy makes. With the knowledge of his strength, dispositions, movements and intentions, you can carefully plot your strategy and when the time is ripe, swoop down and annihilate him at your leisure.

Very early in the space age it was recognized that, in the words of the USAF Manual, "Space is the ultimate high ground". From space you can see the enemy's movement of troops and tanks and planes and rockets and missiles. You can picture his strengths and weaknesses, you can peer into his innermost secrets; you can even eavesdrop into his most intimate conversations.

Since the early 1960s both superpowers have engaged in a race to gain possession of space. For the most part this has consisted in placing satellites in orbit in order to discover what the other side is up to, and to help plan and efficiently execute war on Earth. As Dr Jasani of SIPRI has pointed out against those who claim that satellite surveillance is an essentially peaceful activity, "I cannot for the life of me justify that, for example, a navigation satellite that can guide a weapon to within 10 metres of its target, represents a peaceful activity".

The range and number of military satellites now at the disposal of the two superpowers is awesome indeed. In 1985 it was estimated that over 2,219 satellites had been launched with actual, or potential, military use. This figure represents some 75 per cent of all satellites launched by all nations of the world since the dawning of the space age in 1957. And the number of spacecraft launched for military purposes, is increasing. In 1984 alone, 105 military satellites were placed in orbit by the USSR, USA, China and the European countries of NATO.

The greater number of Soviet military satellite launches has given support to those in the USA who urge that more money be spent on military missions in space. But what is rarely admitted, but must be known by all, is that the life-span of Soviet satellites is very much shorter than that of US spacecraft. The average life ex-

pectancy of a Soviet photo-reconnaissance satellite, for example, is measured in months, sometimes weeks, if not days. The life of US satellites such as KH-11, on the other hand, can be measured in years. Few seriously doubt the immense superiority the United States possesses in terms of satellite technology. The Soviets, for example, still rely heavily upon 'film-return' spy satellites. This means that the film is either processed onboard the spacecraft and the images beamed down to Earth, or alternatively, the film is returned to Earth by capsule for processing. Not only does this entail lengthy delay in receiving information, but the useful life of a satellite is limited by the amount of film it can carry. US satellites, equipped with digital signal transmission can, almost, relay 'pictures' back to base in what American spacemen call 'real time' – that is, live.

The role and capability of each type of military satellite now in service with the two superpowers is a complex and confusing subject. Not only is there little official information available, the names of known satellites can change without notice, so that a satellite may be referred to by several different names. The role and technical capability of a satellite might also be the subject of gross misinformation — much more, or much less, is claimed on its behalf

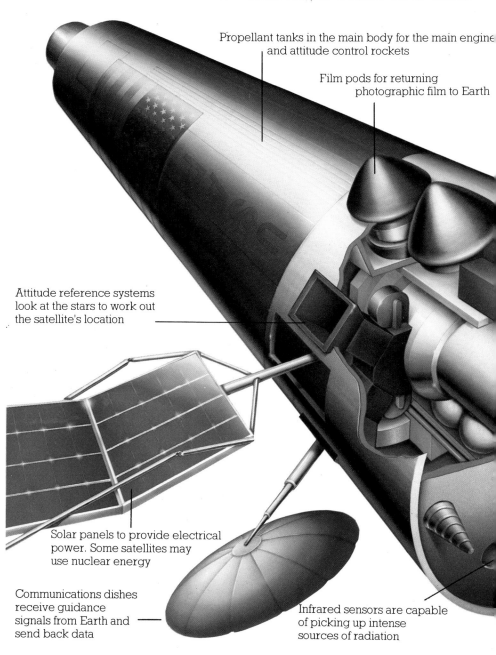

Propellant tanks in the main body for the main engine and attitude control rockets

Film pods for returning photographic film to Earth

Attitude reference systems look at the stars to work out the satellite's location

Solar panels to provide electrical power. Some satellites may use nuclear energy

Communications dishes receive guidance signals from Earth and send back data

Infrared sensors are capable of picking up intense sources of radiation than it is really capable of performing. Much of the equipment carried onboard today's most sophisticated satellites is classified information. In addition to the almost total absence of information about Soviet satellites – reflecting the absence of real information about almost every aspect of Soviet life – there has been a corresponding clampdown recently on certain aspects of the US military space programme, particuarly since the

Below: *In this US spy satellite, the main surveillance system is based on photographic film, but electronic imaging is also used for a 'quick look' facility.*

Large format camera produces highly detailed pictures on photographic film

Quick look camera using electronic imaging systems for an overall view

Above: *The new military shuttle and satellite launch centre 'Slick Six' (Space Launch Complex 6) at Vandenberg Air Force Base.*

Department of Defense (DOD) became involved in space shuttle missions.

From June 1983 a ban has been imposed on information about the orbits of certain US military satellites. As this is one of the ways in which it is possible to identify the true role of a satellite, that task is now much more difficult.

When the useful life of a satellite has been spent, many fall towards Earth and burn up in the atmosphere. But not all. Space is now littered with junk – dead satellites, the upper stages of rockets, discarded protective panels and thousands of fragments resulting from over 75 explosions – both accidental and deliberate. At the end of 1983 NASA's Goddard Space Flight Center at Greenbelt, Maryland, had calculated that over 14,000 man-made objects were careering in orbit around the Earth. On a typical day, NORAD tracks the orbit of some 5,500 objects in space. If an object flies within 80 miles (50km) of a US military satellite USAF Satellite Control Facility at Sunnyvale is alerted of a 'close approach'. 'Collision avoidance' procedure is activated when two objects are within 3-5 miles (5-8km) of each other.

Miraculously, there have been no collisions in geostationary orbit (22,300 miles or 35,880km from Earth), though there have been some catastrophic collisions closer to Earth. When the nuclear-powered Soviet ocean surveillance satellite, Cosmos 954, plummeted to Earth on January 24, 1978, it showered Canada's Northwest Territory with radioactive debris. In operation Morning Light, the Canadian Government, with considerable US assistance, cleaned up the countryside, recovering several kilogrammes of radioactive material spread over a wide area.

In addition to the 14,000 objects logged by NASA, the US Congressional Research Service estimates that there are up to 10,000 fragments too small to be tracked at altitudes of 310-683 miles (500-1,100km). NORAD can track an object as small as 1.5in (4cm) at an altitude of 250 miles

(400km). But in geostationary orbit, an object must be 2¾yd (2.5m) long to be trackable. A tiny metal fragment just 1mm in diameter, travelling at 6¼ miles per second (10km/sec) will penetrate the shell of a satellite. As we shall see, the deliberate scattering of such pellets in space could well be the Soviets' most effective response to the deployment of President Reagan's Strategic Defense system.

With so much debris following so few objects through space it seems almost inevitable that one day a military satellite will be punctured by a flying fragment. What would be the consequences were such a thing to happen? Not knowing that the destruction of one of its military satellites was an 'accident', the superpower concerned might well conclude that it was a deliberate act of aggression. As we have seen, the ability to wage war on Earth is now so dependent upon space systems that it is likely that in any future conflict the first act of hostility will be aimed at the

enemy's command, control, communications and intelligence systems based in space – what is called, in US military jargon, 'C³I' or 'C-cubed I'. As US Air Force Under Secretary Edward Aldridge admits, "Our space systems have become essential to our operational forces. We're going to have to defend them." The deployment in the very near future of a new Anti-Satellite (ASAT) weapons system by the United States (see chapter 2) makes such a scenario even more possible.

Inevitably, the development of such a system will provoke the creation of a counter Soviet ASAT force. Both sides, therefore, will have accepted that a first strike against their satellites is not only possible, but indeed the most likely first act of war. Seemingly threatened by such an attack, the response would be massive nuclear retaliation. With the systems now at the disposal of the superpowers, such a scenario could only too easily become a terrifying reality.

Above: *Worm's eye view of Discovery. Concern that the space shuttle is being used increasingly for military missions is not confined to the Soviets.*

Until recently, satellites made up almost the entire military presence in space. Today there are systems in operation that a few years ago existed only in the realms of science fiction. The space shuttle is such a common image on the television screens in the West, that it is easy to forget how a few years ago such a machine would have been thought technically impossible. Flying its first mission, STS-1, on April 12, 1981, the space shuttle was heralded as man's first step towards exploring the Universe. Cynics in the Kremlin, at the time, tended to pour scorn on the idea, maintaining that the shuttle would be used primarily for military purposes. Few then could have seen into the future. Today, run jointly by NASA and the DOD (Department of Defense), the shuttle plays a major role in the testing of the component parts of SDI.

At the end of 1984, the Department of Defense announced a policy of secrecy surrounding the use of the space shuttle on military missions, though officials admitted that there was little that could be kept from the Russians. "Space is a big place," said a Department of Defense spokesman. "The less they know, the harder it will be for them to find us out there." The new policy was summed up by Brig. Gen. Richard F. Abel, who heads public affairs, USAF; "We intend to protect the identity, mission and all operational details of DOD payloads."

In August 1985 the space shuttle Discovery was launched to rescue the new US Navy communications satellite Leasat F3 which had been launched on April 12, 1985, but had failed to achieve orbit. The shuttle mission also involved the launching of Leasat F4, a spacecraft designed exclusively to be launched from the space shuttle. The design of the shuttle's wings and the size of its cargo bay — capable of carrying twice the payload and three times the volume of the largest rocket launcher — were made to Air Force specification, clearly with a view to future military use. Recently assigned to the newly created Space Command, the space shuttle will form the main space launch vehicle until the 1990s. From spring 1986, "National Security" space shuttle missions, carrying military reconnaissance and meteorological satellites will be launched from the new Space Launch Complex Number 6 — "Slick Six" — at Vandenberg Air Force Base. Here, at Vandenberg, 27 secretly trained military astronauts will work on shuttle missions. Described anonymously by the Department of Defense as "payload specialists", the soldier-spacemen will supervize 37 DOD payloads — 18 of them exclusively military — before September 1988.

Since 1983 the 700 mile (1,125km) range of the shuttle was extended by the use of Boeing Inertial Upper Stage (IUS). This vehicle (17 ft long, 9.5 ft diameter and weighing 32,500lb [5.2m long, 2.9m diameter and weighing 14,742kg]) is carried and launched from the shuttle's roomy cargo bay.

Once detached from the parent shuttle, the IUS is able to place a communications satellite into geo-stationary orbit — 22,300 miles (35,880km) under its own automatic guidance system. Having completed its mission, the spacecraft, in the words of the Boeing Aerospace Company "separates from the satellite (or whatever the payload) and moves to a non-collision position."

The Soviets have been late to develop their own re-usable Space Transportation System. They may have been first in placing a satellite in orbit and putting a man in space, but they have been suspiciously slow in launching a space shuttle, though the DOD claim that a Soviet shuttle is being developed. And, according to US Intelligence reports, a small unmanned scale model of a two-manned Soviet space plane has been test-launched at least three times from the Kapustin Yar missile site on the Volga River, near the Caspian Sea. Achieving low orbit on each occasion, the delta winged spacecraft, bearing a remarkable resemblance to the experimental US space plane, Dyna-Soar, re-entered the atmosphere over the Indian Ocean and was recovered from the sea by Soviet sailors. Analysts at the Pentagon claim that when fully operational, the Soviet plane will play a major 'anti-satellite role', as well as 'the delivery of personnel and components to increasingly sophisticated manned Soviet space complexes'. Salyut 7, the Soviet manned space station, is currently engaged in testing systems and fulfilling military missions. A laser device, able to detect subtle changes on the ocean surface, will, it is claimed, pinpoint the location of submerged US nuclear missile-carrying submarines — now relatively immune from attack. This ability, it is feared, will seriously upset the existing, delicately poised, balance of terror.

Even bigger and better and more powerful manned space stations are being planned by the Soviets for the future, according to the US Department of Defense. In orbit by the 1990s, these permanently manned space stations will be able to spy on US Earth-bound activities at leisure, as well as carrying out tests on sophisticated space weapons systems. They may even be the first move in the creation of manned battle stations beyond the year 2000.

And if the Soviets do that, as the Pentagon fear they will, they will be the first to occupy the "ultimate high ground".

Below: *A scaled-down model of the Soviet* Kosmolyot *— the proposed manned space plane of the future — is recovered from the Indian Ocean.*

CHAPTER 2

'THE BOLT FROM OUT OF THE BLUE'

USAF jargon

"The Air Force will maintain US technological superiority in aerospace and ensure a prolonged war-fighting capability by developing the potential for combat operations in the space medium."

Aerospace: Basic Doctrine, USAF Manual

TWO THOUSAND FEET beneath the granite Cheyenne Mountain, off Colorado Highway 115, lies what could be the last outpost of Western civilization. Behind massive 25-ton doors which the occupants hope will shield them from an all-out nuclear attack, sit 900 men patiently watching tiny television screens. Since 1966 they have sat waiting for Armageddon, or what is known in USAF jargon as a "BOOB" — the bolt from out of the blue. "Buttoned-up", they could hold out for a full 30 days. Today, there is a new mission control centre. Called the Space Defense Operations Center, its task is to track Soviet satellites traversing the globe and to launch, if necessary, an all-out anti-satellite attack.

The call would come, via the hot line, from the President himself. At the word of command, an F-15 Eagle takes off from McChord Air Force Base in Washington state. Zoom climbing to 60,000ft the Eagle unleashes the slim, pointed projectile from under its bulbous belly. Directed by onboard computers, fed with information from space-track stations worldwide, the missile rockets into the abyss. As the target is sighted by the missile's eight infrared telescopes, the warhead separates and its launch vehicle falls to Earth in a ball of fire. No bigger than a soup can, the Miniature Homing Intercept Vehicle (MHIV), twisting twenty revolutions a second, locks on to the target and smashes into it at a speed of 13,716 miles per hour (22,069km/h). The force of the impact produces a blast that shoots thousands of hot metal fragments into the depths of space.

Such a scenario, just a few years ago, existed only in the pages of science fiction. Yesterday's fiction, however, has become today's reality. On Friday September 13, 1985, a twin-tailed F-15 Eagle interceptor took off from a secret airfield somewhere near the western seaboard of the United States. Accelerating to a speed of 1,600 miles per hour, (2,660km/h), at a height of 40,000ft (12,192m), the Eagle unleashed its deadly payload against a 'live', moving, target-satellite. The interception, according to Department of Defense spokesmen, went according to plan.

The acquisition of a new, flexible and sophisticated anti-satellite system was the fulfilment of a secret

report filed in the Pentagon in the winter of 1982/3. Entitled *Fiscal 1984–1988 Defense Guidance*, the document seemed inoccuous enough. Yet its contents make startling and disturbing reading. It reflects the innermost thoughts of top-ranking Pentagon officials and members of the National Security Council within the White House. Within the 136-page document lies a blue print for America's armed forces to prepare to fight a prolonged nuclear war and to wage war in space.

The "development and deployment of a capability to defend space assets is required", reads the report, "as is the capability to deny the enemy the use of his space systems that are harmful to our efforts during conflict". Treaty obligations restricting the deployment of space weapons are brushed aside with the words, "We must ensure that treaties and agreements do not foreclose opportunities to develop these capabilities and systems . . ." In short,

Left: *A US F-15 unleashes its ASAT missile against a 'live' target, September 13, 1985.* Above: *The entrance to NORAD'S mountain redoubt.*

". . . the unique attributes of space will be used . . . to both deter aggression and, should the need arise, to wage war effectively."

With the development of sophisticated military satellites — US armed forces now rely 80 per cent on satellite communications — it was inevitable that anti-satellite (ASAT) weapons would, sooner or later, be developed. Within a few years of the first satellite being launched in October 1957, space engineers, both East and West, were devising ways of shooting them down.

Attempts at creating an effective anti-satellite weapons system have a long and chequered history in the annals of the United States Air Force. Only a few months after the first Sput-

nik had orbited the Earth the USAF was engaged on a research and development programme that was to encounter many of the problems only recently re-discovered by scientists working on Star Wars. Code-named SAINT (Satellite Interceptor) the system was simplicity itself. Thrust into orbit by an Atlas D-Agena B rocket, the satellite interceptor manoeuvred itself into the path of a 'target' satellite by a combination of small propulsion rockets, homing radar and a

television camera. Its task was twofold: to perfect the technique of satellite manoeuvring in space and to carry out detailed inspection of enemy satellite craft. A close encounter with an enemy satellite would result in its interception and destruction.

Initially, SAINT seemed to prosper. Then it became dogged with difficulties. Costs rose, interest flagged until finally the project was shelved. A number of lessons had been learned,

however, that would have to wait another generation before their relevance became clear. One of the most difficult problems SAINT researchers had to solve was how to equip the satellite so that it could spot the difference between a real target and a decoy. To confuse and defeat the system, all the enemy had to do was either overwhelm it — by launching more satellites — or launch a vast number of decoys, or both. It is a simple matter to disguise an orbiting

Island in the Pacific Ocean. The bomb was quite indiscriminate in the trail of devastation it left behind. Emitting high doses of electro-magnetic pulse (EMP), it played havoc with the electronic circuits of passing friendly satellites. It blacked out street lamps, power lines, burglar alarms and most of the telephone system of Honolulu, nearly 1,000 miles (1,609km) to the north – wrecked by high energy electrons flying through space. A similar experiment conducted by one of today's bigger bombs would have even more dramatic results. Detonated above the atmosphere, a space-based nuclear explosion would, according to Arthur C. Clarke, not only knock out *all* orbiting satellites – friend and foe alike – but also have the effect of blacking out the entire power, radio and telephone system of a continent the size of the USA or Europe. "It is something quite new in human history," writes Clarke, "when nations thousands of kilometres from the scene of the conflict could be virtually destroyed in a second *without the loss of a single life.* The dying of course, would start later . . ."

The idea of letting off hydrogen bombs in space seemed a good idea to the two superpowers in the early 1960s. Under the ghoulish codename Squanto Terror (also more prosaically known as Program 437) the USAF set about perfecting an antisatellite system that used nuclear warheads as the "kill mechanism". Johnston Island, a tiny strip of sand one mile long and a quarter of a mile wide (1.6 by 0.4km) was again the chosen test site – mainly because of its remoteness from centres of population and its high security profile. By February 1964 Squanto Terror was ready for action. Mounted on a Thor missile, a MK 49 nuclear warhead could be fired to a maximum altitude of 700 nautical miles (1,296km) and a maximum of 1,500 nautical miles (2,778km) down range. The resulting nuclear blast had a 'satellite killing' range of five nautical miles (8km) which meant that any satellite that

nuclear bomb to make it look like a scientific satellite. Simply 'looking' at a satellite, in any case, does not reveal its identity or purpose. A weapon can easily be covered in dummy casing. It was a problem that the technology at the time had not a hope of solving. But the programme was to prove a useful lesson for projects a generation later – for those prepared to learn from the past.

Even if SAINT had successfully identified and intercepted an enemy

target, it had no means of 'killing' it other than by ramming it at speed – a method still used by some types of Soviet ASAT systems. The first attempts at arming anti-satellite craft were, not surprisingly, closely guarded secrets. Today, their disclosure is enough to make the flesh creep.

On July 8/9, 1962, a single 1.4 megaton nuclear bomb, modest by today's standards, was detonated 250 miles (400km) above Johnston

happened to be within a range of five nautical miles would be destroyed.

On February 15, 1964, a Thor missile, armed with a dummy warhead, rose from its launch pad, climbed to an altitude of 540 nautical miles (1,000km) and at a distance of 443 nautical miles (820km) from Johnston Island successfully intercepted a target. Two more tests, one on March 2, 1964, and another on April 22, 1964, were also successful, with dummy warheads passing close enough to the target for them to have destroyed it. On June 10, 1964, the system was declared officially operational, and 10th Aerospace Defense Squadron USAF, stationed on the island, was put on 24-hour alert with two Thor missiles and their nuclear warheads at the ready.

Sixteen Squanto Terror tests were conducted by the USAF between 1964 and 1968 and despite the 1967 Test Ban Treaty outlawing the use of nuclear weapons in space (though, in fact, the Mk 49 warhead favoured by the system was already prohibited by the 1963 Test Ban Treaty), the programme was kept alive until April 1, 1975. By then it was felt that there was no real threat of the Soviet Union dropping orbiting H-bombs on the United States (a very real fear in the 1960s), and the scientific lesson learned in 1964 – that detonating a nuclear warhead in space was likely to damage US satellites as well as Soviet ones – was more clearly noted. In any case, the system was far too primitive to deal with the vast Soviet military satellite fleet by then orbiting the Earth.

The fear in the early 1960s was that if the Soviets could place a man in a capsule and send him spinning round the globe, they could just as well orbit a nuclear bomb. It was, in fact, a thought that had not only occurred to the Soviets but was one that they were researching and developing. The idea had occurred to the Americans too, but had been firmly rejected by Deputy Defense Secretary Roswell Gilpatric in a speech read and approved by President Kennedy:

The United States believes that it is highly desirable for its own security and for the security of the world that the arms race should not be extended into outer space, and we are seeking in every feasible way to achieve that purpose. Today there is no doubt that either the United States or the Soviet Union could place thermonuclear weapons in orbit, but such an action is just not a rational military strategy for either side for the foreseeable future. We have no program to place any weapons of mass destruction in orbit. An arms race in space will not contribute to our security. I can think of no greater stimulus for a Soviet thermonuclear arms effort in space than a United States commitment to such a program. This we will not do.

When the Soviet orbiting bomb, called the Fractional Orbit Bombardment System, or FOBS, was finally unveiled to the world in November 1967 – by US Secretary of Defense, Robert S. McNamara – the system had already been successfully tested. In January 1967 an SS-9 intercontinental ballistic missile had been fired from the Tyuratum rocket research centre carrying a dummy nuclear warhead. Flying 99.5 miles (160km) over Siberia, the missile had swept over the Pacific, skirted South America, crossed the Atlantic and, heading north over Africa, crossed the Mediterranean before finally re-entering Soviet territory. Moments before completing its orbit, however, the warhead separated and was guided down onto a target. The missile's launch platform then continued its orbit before burning up in the atmosphere in the early hours of the following morning.

The great advantage of the system, from the Soviet point of view, was that it enabled them to deliver hydrogen bombs to the USA by a backdoor route, thus avoiding the elaborate American Ballistic Missile Early Warning System (BMEWS) which monitored the shorter, more direct, North Pole route.

World opinion was naturally outraged by the idea that the Soviets were deploying an orbiting, nuclear bomb in space. Eighteen FOBS in all were deployed at the Tyuratum rocket base – a nominal number – and were tested twice a year until the early 1970s. The prime target, according to Western defence experts, was the US anti-ballistic missile site at Grand Forks Air Force Base, North Dakota; a system that the Americans maintained was in response to the Soviets own ABM deployment. Whatever the truth of the matter (and it has a direct bearing on the later Star Wars programme), FOBS were finally withdrawn by the Soviets in the mid-1970s. By the time the second Strategic Arms Limitation Treaty (SALT II) was signed in Geneva in June 1979, banning FOBS, the system had, as far as is known, been destroyed. Mercifully, the idea of using space bombs lost its appeal in the corridors of power, both East and West, and the threat was over: though there are some in the West who suspect that the Soviets still have FOBS ready and waiting to be used — should the need arise. According to Pentagon reports, leaked to the US press in 1983, the USSR still have all 18 SS-9 FOBS fully operational at their Tyuratum test site. But in the late 1970s attention was diverted to a more pressing need: the development and deployment of other, non-nuclear, anti-satellite weapons.

In the autumn of 1982 Western Intelligence experts formed the firm opinion that the Soviets had, at long last, deployed their much-trumpeted ASAT system. In the early hours of the morning of June 18, 1982, Cosmos 1379 blasted off from Tyuratum cosmodrome in Central Asia into the orbit of Cosmos 1375 — a 'target' satellite launched 12 days earlier, probably from Plesetsk in north west USSR. Under the guidance of ground-control, Cosmos 1379 was manoeuvred on to the flight path of the 'target' satellite, 600 miles (965km) above the Earth. Cosmos 1379 on this occasion flew past its victim and 30 minutes later re-entered the Earth's atmosphere. The demonstration made clear, however, the Soviets' ability to seek out and destroy 'enemy' satellites.

A few hours later two ICBMs, one medium-range SS-20 missile, one submarine-launched ballistic-missile (SLBM) and two anti-ballistic missiles (ABMs) were fired in what came to be known by Western defence analysts as the 'seven hour nuclear war'. The 'war' seemed to confirm the worst fears felt in the West that the Soviets' were preparing to fight a nuclear war, following a scenario that has become familiar. Significantly, the 'war' starts with an attack on low-flying satellites — simulated US spy satellites. Without its spy satellites the US would not know which Soviet missiles had been fired, or be able to locate ballistic missile firing submarines or observe the re-loading of certain nuclear missile silos — factors that are considered by some to be crucial.

After blinding the enemy's 'eyes', the exercise simulated a 'first strike', using ICBMs and IRBMs (Intermediate Range Ballistic Missiles), against selected 'targets' in Europe and the United States. This was followed up swiftly by a more concentrated 'second strike' from submerged submarines. Finally, the exercises tested the Soviets' ability to shoot down incoming, nuclear-tipped ICBMs with X-3 anti-ballistic missiles (ABMs). This, at least, was the view of the exercise taken by the editors of *Aviation Week*. It was also the view taken by the White House. "If war between the superpowers started tomorrow," opined Air Force Secretary Edward Aldridge, "you would see the Soviets employ their ASAT system very rapidly."

Since the late 1960s, when it was first learned that the Soviets were engaged in ASAT research and development ('R & D' in US military jargon), there have been warnings that they were soon to deploy 'hunter-killer' satellites that could shoot US satellites out of the skies in a matter of minutes.

How real is the Soviet threat? Do they, as top US military men insist, really have the ability of destroying America's satellites?

Writing in *Scientific American* in June 1984, three eminent US physicists, Richard L. Garwin (who with Edward Teller and Hans Bethe shares the distinction of having created the world's first H-bomb), Kurt Gottfried and Donald L. Hafner, take America's top brass to task. Closely analyzing all the available evidence (which, as with everything concerning the Soviet Union, is necessarily incomplete), they came to a conclusion that is at odds with official US government statements. Piecing together the findings of Garwin, Gottfried and

Below: *The Soviet ASAT interceptor launch site at Tyuratum. Experts claim this system is a generation behind the US F-15 ASAT.*

Hafner with other available information, the following features about the Soviet ASAT system emerge:

● The Chinese have more to fear from the Soviet ASATs than does the United States because few US satellites follow the inclination of the Soviet ASATs' flight path – between 62 and 65 degrees with respect to the Equator. Chinese satellites *do* follow such a course. Indeed, there are many parallels between the launches and orbits of Chinese satellites and Soviet ASAT tests.

● The Soviet ASAT weapon is launched by a massive booster rocket, a modified SS-19 ICBM – about the length of three buses parked end to end. It is impossible to launch the missile without lengthy preparation. There are also few launch sites in the Soviet Union capable of handling these giant, liquid-fuelled rockets. So it would be impossible for the Soviets to 'take out' America's military satellites suddenly, without the US knowing.

● The highest altitude reached by Soviet ASATs in tests has been about 14,913 miles (24,000km) – far below the orbits of US navigation, early-warning (EW) and vital communications satellites. Most US spy

and US Navy ocean reconnaissance satellites would, however, be vulnerable to attack. The SDS strategic communications satellite system – upon which so much depends – *does* fly at an inclination of 63 degrees, but as it passes the Earth at its perigee it would hurtle past a Soviet ASAT 1,000 mph (1,609km/h) faster.

● The Soviet ASAT system enables a satellite to be attacked only when its ground track passes close to the launch site of the ASAT weapon. This happens only twice a day.

● The Soviets have encountered many difficulties in perfecting a workable target-finding device – the first essential in successful hunter satellite killing. US intelligence maintains that the one currently in use is 'not very impressive'.

In the tests conducted between 1968 and 1971, directing the 'killersat' on to the target was achieved by radar. The 'interceptor' satellite impacted with the target after two complete orbits. In later tests, a radar-directed homing device was used, and interception occurred after only one orbit. The system achieved a 50 per cent success rate. Further tests were also conducted using an optical-infrared homing

device. But in all six tests carried out using the system, not one succeeded in locating the target.

Together, these factors indicate that it would take the Soviets, using their available ASAT system, several weeks to destroy all 18 US military satellites, now *within its range.*

At the end of their report, Garwin, Gottfried and Hafner conclude that the "Current Russian ASAT system presents a ponderous, inflexible and quite limited threat to us". And they quote with approval Air Force Chief of Staff, General Lew Allen Jr.,

---

"I think our general opinion is that we give it [the Soviet ASAT system] a very questionable operational capability for a few launches. In other words, it is a threat we are worried about, but they have not had a test program that would cause us to believe it is a very credible threat."

"Nothing", add the three physicists "has happened since 1979 [when the statement was made] to change this assessment."

The view of President Reagan is, however, somewhat different. Speaking at Edwards Air Force Base a month after the 'seven hour nuclear war', the President reaffirmed America's commitment to deploy a new ASAT system as soon as possible. Tough talking is the President's style, and on this occasion the talk was soon matched by some tough action. In the autumn of that year, 1982, it was officially announced that a special force had been created to test a new generation of US anti-satellite weapons.

The show-piece in this arsenal is the Miniature Homing Intercept Vehicle (MHIV), launched from an F-15 fighter. The two-stage rocket propels the vehicle into space at a speed of 10,000 mph (16,093km/h). Guided by eight infrared sensors, the 'warhead' locks on to the target. The manoeuvre is made by the firing of fifty-six tiny rockets which thrust the

Left: *A US DOD artist's impression of the Soviet 'hunter-killer' anti-satellite (ASAT) interceptor, in operation today. Few experts believe it poses a serious threat.*

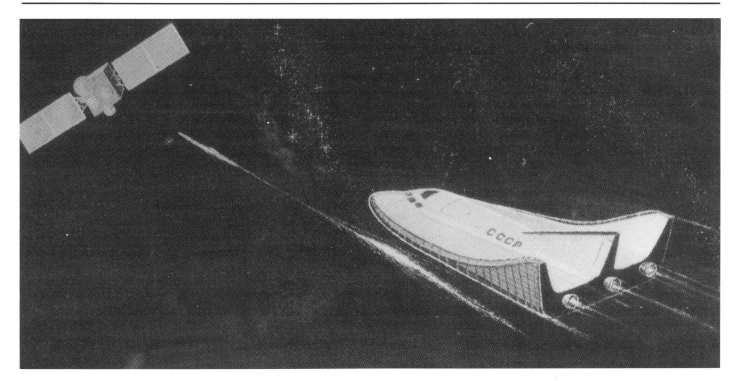

warhead headlong on to the target which is destroyed by the force of the impact (kinetic energy).

Work on the F-15 began in 1978. Scheduled to be fully operational in 1987, the progress of the weapon's development has closely followed the tortuous state of East-West relations in recent years. When relations seemed to be improving, the importance of the weapon was downgraded; with a cooling of relations, particularly since the return of Ronald Reagan to the White House, development and deployment became more urgent. The weapon itself came to be seen as a useful bargaining counter with which to cajole the Soviets into making concessions that they might not otherwise make. This certainly seemed to be the view of the Reagan Administration in September 1985 when the weapon was tested against a live target for the first time. Despite warnings from Moscow that such a test would lead to their developing and deploying new ASAT weapons — leading to a fresh arms race in space — the test went ahead, nevertheless. Authorizing the action on August 20, 1985, a spokesman for the President, who was holidaying on his Californian ranch, said simply: "We have to test, and test now." In response, the Soviet news agency *Tass* denounced the exercise as "nothing but an action directly leading to the commencement of the deployment of a new class of dangerous armaments —

strike space weapons".

To the editors of *Time* magazine, Soviet leader Mikhail Gorbachev repeated a claim often heard from the Soviets: that there is a direct link between the testing of the US ASAT system and the development of President Reagan's Star Wars. "The very fact," warned Party Secretary Gorbachev, "that the US is now planning to test a second generation anti-satellite system is fraught with the most serious consequences. We will surely act. This test . . . means in fact testing an element of a space-based ABM [anti-ballistic missile]."

What form a new generation of Soviet ASATs may take became a matter of keen interest in the Western press in the summer of 1985. Some said the Russians would strew space with mines. Others claimed that the Soviets already possessed ground-based lasers that could 'zap' American satellites — even missiles — whenever they wanted. Suddenly, Soviet technology was so sophisticated that it was credited with being able to devise the most fiendish weapons, almost overnight.

In this vein, commentators were fed with information from various official sources in the United States. In its annual review of *Soviet Military Power 1985,* the Department of Defense claimed that the Soviet "directed-energy development programs involve future Ballistic Missile Defense (BDM) as well as anti-

Above: *The Soviet space plane Kosmolyot of the future will, US Intelligence fear, have an ASAT operational role. Scaled models have already been tested.*

satellite and air-defense weapons concepts."

"By the late 1980s," claims the review, "the Soviets could have prototypes for ground-based lasers . . . Testing of the components for a large-scale deployment system could begin in the early 1990s. . . In the late 1980s, they could have prototype space-based laser weapons for use against satellites. In addition, ongoing Soviet programs have progressed to the point where they could include construction of ground-based laser anti-satellite (ASAT) facilities at operational sites. These could be available by the end of the 1980s and would greatly increase the Soviets' laser ASAT capability beyond that currently at their test site at Sary Shagan. They may deploy operational systems of space-based lasers for anti-satellite purposes in the 1990s, if their technology developments prove successful, and they can be expected to pursue development of space-based laser systems for ballistic missile defense for possible deployment after the year 2000."

The review lists other developments the Soviets have been engaged in — all aimed at showing how advanced the Soviets are in the space arms race, and how the US is being left woefully behind. "Since the 1970s", it is stated, "the Soviets have had a research program to explore the technical feasibility of a particle beam weapon in space. A prototype space-based particle beam weapon intended only to disrupt satellite electronic equipment could be tested in the early 1990s. One designed to destroy satellites could be tested in space in the mid-1990s."

Fleshing out the Gorbachev claim that the US deployment of its F-15 ASAT system would lead to a new ASAT arms race seems to mean that the following weapons systems will be developed and deployed:

Space-based kinetic energy weapons
Ground and space-based laser weapons
Ground and space-based particle beam weapons
Ground and space-based radiofrequency weapons

As we shall see in Chapter 4, these systems form essential elements in the Star Wars programme.

Reports that the Soviets have achieved the capability to wage war in space are not new. *Aviation Week*, in the autumn of 1981, claimed – based, it was said, on an intelligence leak – that Cosmos 1267 was ". . . equipped with firing ports to eject 1-meter-long miniature vehicles guided by infrared sensors . . . Docking of this anti-satellite weapon platform with Salyut 6 (the Soviet space station) means the USSR would be able to use a manned Salyut 6 to direct anti-satellite attacks against US spacecraft or to protect Soviet satellites against a US retaliatory attack."

The report was discounted and derided by informed analysts. It was very doubtful that the Soviets possessed even the technology to find US satellites in space, let alone the ability to direct anti-satellite weapons to kill such targets. Such a development seemed unlikely given that the only known operational Soviet ASAT system was described by one US expert as an 'old blunderbuss'.

In any case, a rocket only 1 metre long would not be able to travel far from the parent craft: it could only be

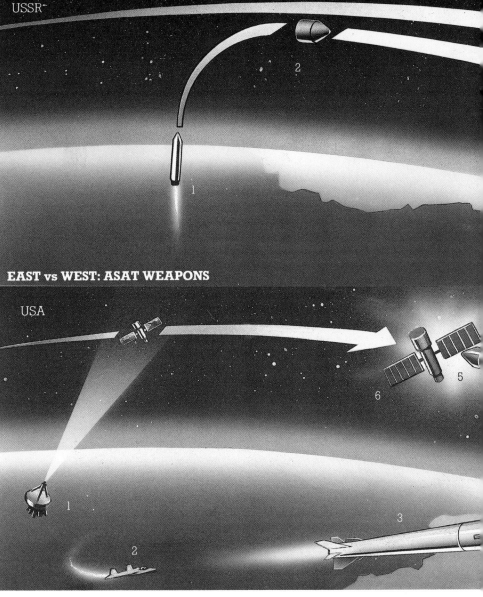

EAST vs WEST: ASAT WEAPONS

used as a defensive weapon.

That research has and is being conducted into the use of high-tech weapons to be used against satellites – in both the USA and the Soviet Union – is undoubtedly true. But the ability of either country to deploy such systems in the immediate future seems, on the evidence, to be most unlikely.

In Chapter 4 we shall be looking in detail at the technological problems that Star Wars scientists have encountered, and will have to overcome, before their system could, literally, get off the ground. An anti-satellite weapons system on a scale envisaged by the DOD would suffer exactly the same problems. And there is nothing to suggest that these are problems that the Soviets have already overcome.

Top: *A rocket (1) launches the ASAT warhead (2) into orbit. Following the path of its prey, the warhead closes in and is detonated (4).* Above: *Tracking stations (1) plot the course of alien satellite (6). An F-15 interceptor (2) fires its ASAT missile (3) which is directed to the target by onboard computers. The warhead (4) locks onto the satellite (5) and the MHIV destroys it by smashing into the target (5).*

Pentagon planners have looked hard and long for at least the last 20 years at ways of shooting down Soviet satellites. As we have seen, early attempts concentrated on nuclear explosions emitting highly lethal doses of EMP (electro-magnetic pulse). Today, the Bomb is being

Above: *DARPA director Robert Cooper.*

"The material is very promising for application to our own strategic [nuclear missile and space] systems to protect them against potential laser damage." The fabric is said to be some 100 times stronger than anything currently used. The material has to be light, otherwise the payload it protects would be too heavy to carry into space by current launch vehicles. Cooper claims that the "secret graphite coating" would form "perhaps 10 per cent of [the] payload", presumably an acceptable figure, and "can withstand perhaps as much as an order of magnitude (10 times), or two (100 times) more energy deposited on it in the way of laser radiation than the typical aerospace material".

The spawning of new ways of killing a satellite has also spawned a new industry and a brand-new technology. Called, cryptically, in US military jargon, 'satellite survivability', it also has had direct application to Star Wars. If the 'secret graphite coating' can protect satellites against most forms of assault, could such a substance not be used to protect missiles against the sort of defences used in the Star Wars programme? What if the Soviets covered their ICBMs with the 'secret graphite coating', would that not make them immune to everything that Star Wars could hurl at them? Emphatically not, says Cooper. In any case, he claims, the Soviets just haven't the technology to create such a substance. Soviet technology, it seems, is curiously strong in those areas in which the US is deficient, yet fortunately weak in those areas where it is claimed the US is strong.

The preoccupation of ensuring 'satellite survivability' against nuclear radiation is possibly unnecessary. Nothing has changed to alter the fact that nuclear bursts are just as likely to destroy friendly satellites as they are enemy ones.

A more fruitful line of research is the more traditional one of electronic jamming. Electronic circuitry onboard today's military satellites is highly sensitive and very vulnerable. This weakness has led to the development of a sophisticated game involving all sorts of scientific wizardry. The creation of electronic warfare weapons (EW) has in turn led to electronic countermeasures, leading to fresh electronic counter-counter-

looked at again as a possible ASAT weapon. This time interest focuses on channeling X-rays on to a target satellite in order to produce what scientists call 'System Generated Electromagnetic Pulse'. Afflicted with this condition, a satellite overloads and burns out. Such tests that have been conducted have shown just how big a dose a satellite can take of EMP and what materials might be used to 'harden' them against nuclear explosions. From the military's point of view, it is vital that in the event of a general nuclear war its satellites continue to function. Materials such as light, carbon fabrics are being tested to provide the necessary protection against nuclear radiation.

According to Robert Cooper, director of DARPA (Defense Advanced Research Projects Agency),

measures, . . . and so on.

Little is known of this area of weapons research and development, and virtually nothing about Soviet electronic warfare weapons. Nevertheless, the USAF's Space Command assume a Soviet capability in this area because they are setting about the expensive job of encrypting their radio signals and making them resistant to jamming. Other ways of defeating EW is to make the satellite less dependent on ground stations for instructions. This has led to research into what is known as 'satellite autonomy'.

Another threat to satellite survival is posed by the 'space mine' – a device that some have claimed the Soviets already possess. Rather like the naval mine developed in the last century, the space mine is, however, sown deep in space – geostationary orbit presents an ideal environment because it poses the greatest possible threat to vital space traffic: communications, early-warning and intelligence satellites. A mine placed here could also be safely slotted into orbit until it was ready to be used. At the flick of a switch it could be manoeuvred onto the path of the approaching target. Such a weapon would not be easy to detect – it could easily be made to look like an innocent scientific spacecraft. There is little a nation could do to protect its satellites against such a device, short of hardening their satellites or manoeuvring them out of the way once it was realized they were under attack.

Pentagon claims that the Soviets have a ground-based laser gun capable of blinding US satellites, gained certain credibility in 1975 when it was reported that a US early-warning satellite had fallen foul of such a device. Reports that the failure of the

**WAR IN SPACE:
GROUND INSTALLATIONS**

USA

1 McChord AFB, Washington. Proposed F-15 ASAT air base.
2 Lawrence Livermore National Laboratory.
3 Vandenberg AFB, California. Space Launch Complex
   Six (military shuttle launch centre); military
   satellite launch site; ASAT test range.
4 San Juan, Capistiano, California. US Navy laser test range.
5 NORAD HQ, Cheyenne Mountain, Colorado.
6 Los Alamos Laboratory, New Mexico. Major particle
   beam weapon laboratory.
7 USAF Weapons Laboratory, New Mexico.
8 White Sands, New Mexico. GEODSS station; High
   Energy Laser National Test Range.
9 Grand Forks AFB, North Dakota. Abandoned Safeguard
   ABM site.
10 Cape Canaveral, Florida. Major launch center
   for early shuttle missions and military satellites.
11 Langley, Virginia. CIA Operations Center; second
   USAF F-15 ASAT base.
12 Johnston Island. ASAT 'Squanto Terror'
   test area.
13 Kwajalein Atoll. ASAT and HOE test site.

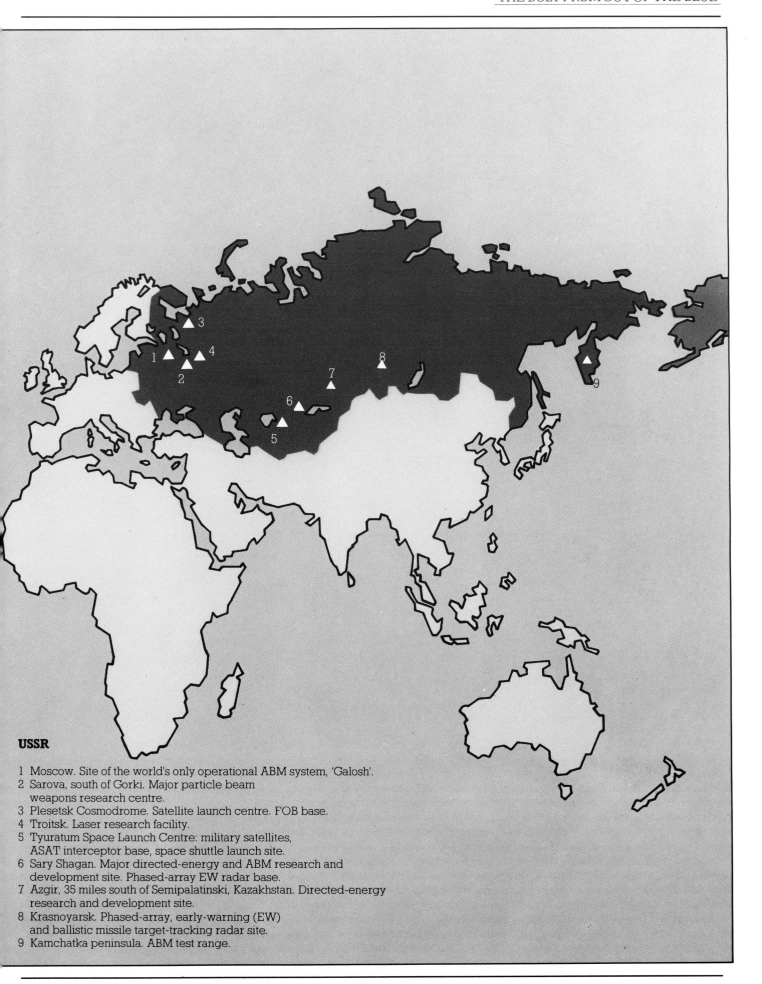

USSR

1 Moscow. Site of the world's only operational ABM system, 'Galosh'.
2 Sarova, south of Gorki. Major particle beam
  weapons research centre.
3 Plesetsk Cosmodrome. Satellite launch centre. FOB base.
4 Troitsk. Laser research facility.
5 Tyuratum Space Launch Centre: military satellites,
  ASAT interceptor base, space shuttle launch site.
6 Sary Shagan. Major directed-energy and ABM research and
  development site. Phased-array EW radar base.
7 Azgir, 35 miles south of Semipalatinski, Kazakhstan. Directed-energy
  research and development site.
8 Krasnoyarsk. Phased-array, early-warning (EW)
  and ballistic missile target-tracking radar site.
9 Kamchatka peninsula. ABM test range.

satellite's infrared sensors had been caused by gas-field fires in the Soviet Union, did not convince everyone. Then, in 1980, a CIA report, discounted by the Pentagon, but accepted by *Aviation Week,* claimed that the Soviets did have a ground-based high-energy laser gun in operation capable of shooting down US satellites in low-Earth orbit.

A laser based on the ground (as will be seen in Chapter 4) is, in any case, a weapon of limited use. Laser beams aimed at objects in space would have to pass through the atmosphere. This diffuses their intensity, thus making them considerably less effective. To hit a target and destroy it would require hitting the target's sensors precisely as it passed over. Counter-measures to protect space craft lasers are, in any case, relatively cheap and simple. Special filters covering the satellite's sensors could reject the laser's wavelength, rendering the beam impotent. According to one expert on anti-satellite weapon technology, laser hardening and sensor protection 'is nearly perfected for defensive applications'.

The prospect of curbing the use of space as a battlefield in the future seems remote, though politicians, both East and West, pay homage to such a hope. Increasingly, however, to many in the present US Administration, talk of banning the research, development of deployment of ASAT weapons is dismissed as folly. The official line adopted by the Administration was aired in March 1983 by George Keyworth. "If we could con-

ceive of a treaty with the Soviet Union that was truly verifiable . . . that would be one issue. [But] it is an almost impossible thing to do in space."

To the hawks, however, any treaty banning the use of ASAT weapons, even if it was verifiable, is bad in principle. This view is certainly one

Below: *An artist's impression of the upper stage (containing the MHIV) of the USAF's ASAT missile launched by the F-15 Eagle, left.*

held by Richard N. Perle, Assistant Secretary of Defense for International Security. Voicing a feeling that has found favour in the White House, Perle believes that even if an ASAT treaty was verifiable he was against it because it would give "sanctuary" to Soviet satellites to spy on US military activity. "Verification" it seems has become no more than a smoke-screen.

In November 1983 the National Council of the Federation of American Scientists expressed the same

fear in a report in which they said: "It is difficult to avoid the impression that the Administration is simply not interested in an arms control option in this area and intends to proceed with deployment, regardless of the alternatives and consequences."

Even if one were to ignore the fact that the Soviet ASAT system is a fairly primitive weapon, the authors of the report state that it is not true that an ASAT weapons treaty cannot be monitored or verified. And the reasons for this are simple:

1. The size of the Soviet ASAT booster rocket – the SS-9 ICBM – is so massive that it is impossible to conceal its launch.
2. Once the weapon has been placed in orbit, its progress is easily tracked by ground stations.
3. Even if the Soviets were to break an ASAT treaty limiting the number of weapons each side could operate, they could not test any additional weapons without the US knowing. A report published in *Aviation Week & Space Technology*, March 28, 1983, confirmed the view that there is little the Soviets can do in space without the US knowing about it. From the Space Defense Operations Center, Soviet ASAT launches are monitored, "even," in the words of the report, "if it appears the Soviets are going after one of their own target spacecraft, the Center . . . alerts all US satellite operators with vehicles in orbits that could be reached by the Soviet ASAT as it flies its mission."
4. The testing and deployment of more sophisticated ASAT weapons systems would be equally impossible without the US knowing. Space-based lasers, for example, can be easily spotted because of their huge mirrors. 'Space mines' might be deployed disguised as satellites and avoid detection, but the placing of vast "space mine fields" on a scale necessary to knock out all US satellites, could not be done covertly.

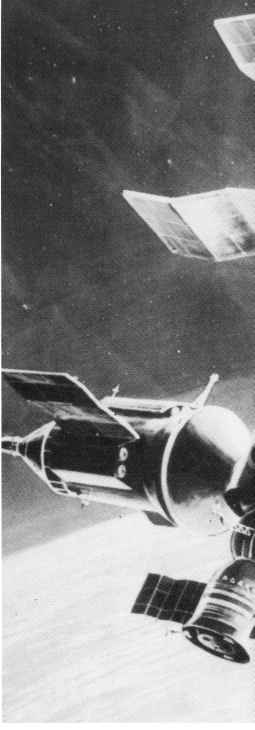

Above: A bolt from the blue. The US ASAT missile, directed by on-board computers, rockets to its target-satellite.

The real reason why President Reagan seems reluctant to negotiate a ban on ASAT weapons, says the Federation, is because such a ban would cancel research, development and deployment of Star Wars. Ground-based lasers and space-based weapons would be banned by any ASAT treaty – they are obviously capable of being used as anti-satellite weapons. But they are also essential features of the President's Star Wars anti-ballistic missile defensive system. Understandably, an ASAT test ban treaty would effectively wreck the President's scheme.

For two years the message from the Kremlin was broadcast to the world, loud and clear. While *they*, the Soviets, were placing a moratorium on the testing of ASAT weapons, the Americans continued to test. From the beginning of 1983 to the end of 1984 hardly a speech was made by a Soviet leader addressed to the West, in which a plea was not made to ban the testing of ASAT weapons. Then, just days before US Secretary of State George Shultz was due to meet Soviet Minister Andrei Gromyko in Geneva in January 1985, the talking suddenly stopped. The US negotiating team flew to Geneva well-primed to

answer Soviet accusations. Not only were no such accusations made, the Soviets did not mention the subject at all. The US team was unnerved. Said one astonished spokesman, "It was the dog that didn't bark in the night. We couldn't believe it." Hurriedly, experts combed the fine print of the Soviet text. Apart from one or two slight references, the subject had mysteriously been dropped from the Soviet agenda. What, the Americans wondered, were the Soviets up to?

The answer, when it came, was not to the President's liking. Tired of talking, the Soviets had given up on banning ASAT weapons and decided to act on the principle: if you can't beat them, join them. According to reports, the Soviets had embarked on a programme of replacing their antiquated ASAT system with a new, top secret programme: one that would match, if not surpass the one the Americans were about to deploy. That, at least, is what the Kremlin wished the White

Above: *The shape of things to come? The Soviet space shuttle delivers personnel and components to a manned space station of the future.*

House to believe. If it was true – if the Russians really were developing new ASAT weapons – what was there to stop them using these weapons against Star Wars? From the White House's point of view, things were going dangerously wrong.

CHAPTER 3

'THE MAGINOT LINE OF THE 21st CENTURY'

Sir Geoffrey Howe, British Foreign Secretary, March 23, 1985

"It is the business opportunity of a generation...
the scramble for that pot of gold is on."

Wall Street Journal

THE IDEA OF SHOOTING down an inter-continental ballistic missile armed with a nuclear warhead before it reaches its target, is not new. As long ago as 1955, two full years before the Soviets announced that they had nuclear-armed ICBMs, US Army scientists were working out ways of successfully intercepting and destroying them. Their efforts resulted in the Nike-Zeus anti-ballistic missile. The Nike-Zeus is interesting because it shows clearly how an anti-ballistic missile can also, quite easily, be adapted and used as an anti-satellite weapon. In the case of the Nike-Zeus, which began life under the official designation 'Program 505', though designed as an ABM, was eventually deployed and found operational status as an anti-satellite weapon.

Technically, an anti-ballistic missile is not very different from an anti-satellite missile. Their function is similar: to intercept and destroy a moving target in space. Both must be ready for action at a moment's notice. But there are differences, though these are small. And the differences are a result of their different targets. An ICBM follows a descending trajectory, while that of a satellite is, roughly, horizontal. Consequently, the programmed guidance system — calculating the angle, speed and distance of the target — used by an ASAT missile is different from that of an ABM missile. But the major difference is that while the ASAT missile is presented with just one target — an orbiting satellite — an ABM missile may have to contend with a large number of 'targets' thrown up by the enemy to confuse the defensive system. These may consist of trying to overwhelm the defence by presenting multiple targets, the use of decoys, 'chaff', electronic jamming, flying booster debris, or any number of these counter-measures together.

Although primitive by today's standards, the Nike-Zeus was nevertheless an impressive weapon. Standing some 50ft (15m) off the ground, it consisted of a three-stage rocket and a 'nose' or 'jethead' capable of carrying a 1-megaton thermonuclear warhead. First launched successfully on December 16, 1959, it was deployed as an anti-satellite weapon on Kwajalein Atoll, in the Pacific Ocean, in 1962, armed with a nuclear warhead. The deployment of the

Nike-Zeus as an ASAT weapon, however, was not the end of research into ABM defence. With hindsight the mid-1950s can be seen to have been crucial to the way in which the world was to evolve over the next three decades. This was clearly recognized by US President Dwight D. Eisenhower. Writing on April 12, 1956, Eisenhower stated that:
". . . the true security problem of the day . . . is not merely man against man or nation against nation. It is man against war . . . When we get to

Left: *A Spartan ABM missile launch, 1969.* Above: *The Nike-Zeus ABM/ASAT facility at White Sands, New Mexico.*

the point, as one day we will, that both sides know that in any outbreak of general hostilities, regardless of the element of surprise, destruction will be both reciprocal and complete, possibly we will have sense enough to meet at the conference table with the understanding that the era of

armaments has ended and the human race must conform its actions to this truth or die."

Though both sides possessed the hydrogen bomb at the time, neither side had the means of launching a missile, armed with a nuclear warhead, across continents direct to the other's cities and missile silos. The only means of delivering hydrogen bombs was by the conventional, heavy bomber. This was to the USSR's disadvantage. While the USA ringed the USSR with bomber bases on almost all her borders, the only way the Soviets had of striking deep into the American heartland was by the long and hazardous intercontinental route. It was a state of affairs not to the Soviet's liking. Nevertheless, the bomber, from a political point of view, did have one major advantage over the ICBM: it was recallable. It permitted politicians to change their minds about the wisdom of 'nuking' the other side. It also allowed for 'mistakes' to be rectified before it was too late. Today, when the button is pressed, there is no turning back.

There is nothing to stop the terrible inevitability of total destruction.

Anxious to overcome what they perceived as vulnerability, the Soviets – or so the Americans believed at the time – threw all their resources into developing a rocket programme that would enable them to launch a massive missile strike against the North American continent. By the time John F. Kennedy became president of the United States in November 1960, the Pentagon, the State Department and the White House were convinced that the Soviets enjoyed a clear superiority in numbers of missiles. This was the 'missile gap' about which so much was said and written and debated in the early 1960s. It was a major feature of the Kennedy election campaign and a major feature of his Administration's defence policy: to engage in a re-armament programme in order to reverse the Soviet's superiority. Tens of thousands of people were drawn into the enterprise and millions of dollars were spent on developing America's ICBM

Left: *The militarization of space began under President Eisenhower.* Top: *Claiming the Russians to be ahead of the US in ICBMs, President Kennedy began an arms race that has continued to this day. His successor, Lyndon B. Johnson (above) was later to admit that this was a mistake.*

arsenal. And when it was revealed by spy satellites that the missile gap was a total *illusion* – that, in fact, not only did the Soviet's not enjoy a clear lead in numbers of missiles, but that their ICBMs were few in number and technologically inferior to the Americans' – there was nothing that could be done to stop the process of re-armament. The Americans, it was realized, had been completely taken in by Russian propaganda.

The role of the military spy satellite showed what only years later President Lyndon B. Johnson was to admit in public:

"We were doing things we didn't need to do, we were building things we didn't need to build; we were harboring fears we didn't need to harbor."

It was two years after the US government had set in motion a programme of nuclear missile production that the full inventory of Soviet missile strength was gathered by US close-look and area-survey satellites. By then there was no turning back. Acting on false information, President Kennedy had set in train a war machine that was to threaten the stability of the world for many years. By 1962, two years after Kennedy became President, the US had over 400 intercontinental ballistic missiles armed with nuclear warheads, *more* than they had two years previously. Russia, at the time, had less than 80. And the process that Kennedy had set in motion in 1960 was inexorable. By

1968, the US strategic nuclear force comprised 1,710 land- and sea-based missiles. The Soviets, after a late start — in 1969 they had fewer than 1,000 missiles — continued production, long after the US had stopped. In 1971 they reached and surpassed the US total. But not only did the number of missiles increase. With the miniaturization of nuclear warheads, the number each missile could carry also increased. In the early 1970s, a device called the Multiple Independently-Targeted Re-entry Vehicle, or MIRV, added a new concept to the grisly game of the nuclear arms race.

An ICBM follows through four phases from the moment it is launched to the point when it reaches its target. The first phase, known as the 'boost phase' launches the missile

some 100km or more into space by powerful multistage booster rockets. The next stage, the 'post-boost' phase, consists in the MIRVs separating from the booster rocket and manoeuvring themselves on to the target course. In the third, or 'mid-course' phase MIRVs follow an essentially identical ballistic trajectory until they reach the fourth, aptly named, 'terminal phase', when the warheads re-enter the atmosphere on to the target.The flight time for current ICBMs launched from ground-based missile silos in the Soviet Union to

Below: *A technician supervises the positioning of a fifth nuclear warhead onto the deployment module of an MX missile. The MX is designed specifically to attack hard targets.*

targets in the United States, is between 25 and 30 minutes; for submarine-launched ballistic missiles (SLBMs) stationed off the US coast, the time taken to target is a mere ten minutes. Each MIRV or 'bus', carries 10 or more independently-targeted nuclear warheads, each representing a destructive power many hundreds of times greater than that contained in the two atomic bombs dropped over Japan in 1945.

In theory, the value of this new weapon was that it strengthened deterrence because instead of being aimed at big civilian cities and centres of communication and command — so-called 'soft targets' — the new, smaller, more accurate nuclear warheads, could be targeted more precisely against 'hard targets' such as Soviet ICBM silos. This would effectively contain the Soviets' ability to wage prolonged nuclear war — or so it was argued. In fact, the development and deployment of MIRVs led to a fresh arms race and a greater number of nuclear *warheads* being deployed. The beauty of the system, from the military's point of view, was that more warheads could be bought without the expense of buying more missiles. By the end of the 1970s, the United States was equipped with over 7,000 nuclear warheads. Today, the number stands at 26,000.

Naturally the Soviets were not slow to develop and deploy their own MIRV system, fearful of being 'left behind' in the strategic arms race. And when the Soviets began experimenting with various anti-ballistic missile defence systems — as they did in the 1960s and '70s — the US response was to build even more nuclear warheads to overwhelm it. So began yet another round in the gruesome contest of nuclear parity. Attempts to contain or even reverse the process have done little to reduce the actual number of nuclear warheads each side owns. Since the signing of the Strategic Arms Limitation Talks agreement, SALT I, in May 1972, the nuclear arsenal of both superpowers has *increased*. Though both sides agreed to limit the number of missiles capa-

In the ever-increasing nuclear arms race between the two super-powers, Trident, right, has added yet another dimension to mass destruction.

ble of delivering nuclear warheads to each other to 2,400, the agreement did nothing to limit the number of warheads. So production of MIRVs and MRVs – Multiple Re-entry Vehicles – continued. New systems and new weapons have now been added, partly to replace the, by now, ageing weapons at the superpowers' disposal, and partly in response to technological advances. Thus a new list of names has entered into the language of mass destruction – SS-20s, Pershing II, Trident, air-launched, sea-launched and ground-launched cruise missiles, the B-1 bomber, and the MX (also called, ironically, the 'Peacemaker') missile.

With each delivery system capable of carrying many nuclear warheads, this represents (approximately) a total of 10,770 nuclear warheads (including MIRVs) and bombs for the

Below: *Soviet deployment of the SS-20 long-range missile convinced many in the US of the need for Star Wars.*

By the end of 1985 the nuclear weapons (launchers and warheads) at the disposal of the superpowers was as follows:

	USA	USSR
LAUNCHERS		
Land-based	1030	1398
Submarine-based	592	946
Bombers	297	303
TOTAL	1919	2647
WARHEADS AND BOMBS		
Land-based ICBMs	2130	6420
Submarine-Launched	5344	2122
Bombs, Air-to-surface missiles, Air-launched cruise	3296	1052
TOTAL	10,770	9594

Above: *The building of the Safeguard ABM system at Grand Forks AFB, North Dakota, went ahead despite opposition. But the day after it opened Congress closed it down.*

United States, and 9,594 warheads (including MIRVs) and bombs for the Soviet Union.

Against this frightening background and the failure of any real reductions being made in the number of nuclear warheads stockpiled in the world today, it is not surprising that from time to time over the past thirty years, politicians' thoughts (and those of the military too) have turned to creating an effective defence against nuclear ballistic missiles.

Although there are some who say that the only effective defence against nuclear attack is to ensure that it never happens (and this is a topic to which we shall be returning), there are those (and they are in a majority in the White House today) who are not interested, it seems, in *any* agreement. Their view of the way out of the current danger is quite different. And it is based on two basic premises.

1. That the United States must again achieve nuclear superiority over the Soviet Union and regain the position it had enjoyed for a short time in the 1960s.

2. If war comes, the United States must be prepared for its own (and possibly that of its Allies') survival.

The question of whether nuclear war is survivable has been answered many times by different members of the Reagan Administration clearly and unequivocally. Indeed, there are those who think that nuclear war might even be a good thing. Conspicuous among this group is the US's

chief disarmament spokesman, Eugene Rostow, Director of US Arms Control and Disarmament Agency. "Japan, after all," says Rostow, "not only survived but flourished after the nuclear attack." It is against this background that the whole question of anti-ballistic missile (ABM) defences must be seen — and Star Wars, or the Strategic Defense Initiative, is essentially a new form of anti-ballistic missile defence.

Several attempts have been made by both superpowers to erect an ABM defence system since the 1960s. With the transfer of the Nike-Zeus anti-ballistic missile to an anti-satellite role in the late 1950s, the US anti-ballistic missile programme was re-structured, reorganized and given a fresh face. Code-named Sentinel, the project prospered under the Presidency of Richard Nixon. It aimed at providing for the defence of America's cities against nuclear attack by using two interceptor missiles, Spartan and Sprint. Spartan was the larger of the two. Its role was to intercept incoming ICBMs before they re-entered the atmosphere and destroy them with a thermonuclear warhead. Those missiles Spartan missed were to be eliminated by the fast accelerating, two-stage Sprint,

which was launched from underground silos and destroyed its victim by means of a 'low-yield' nuclear explosion.

Nixon's attempt to get Congress to agree to the deployment of Sentinel failed for three reasons. First, because of growing anti-Nixon feeling in the country, so that anything Nixon was in favour of, many were against; second, environmental — not many people were happy with the idea of having their cities ringed with nuclear-tipped missiles; and third, technical — few people believed that the system would defend them against an all-out nuclear attack.

Having failed with Sentinel, Nixon tried again by renaming the project Safeguard and proposing instead of an all-embracing ABM system aimed at defending people, a defence of America's ICBM silos against a pos-

Below: *The ballistic missile defences around Moscow rely on the ageing ABM interceptor Galosh (right). By 1987 it will be replaced by the new SA-X-3.*

Moscow

ABM Radar

ABM Rada

ABM-1B Complex _____
ABM Silo Sites Under Co
Roads _____

sible Soviet first strike. Work began on the deployment of two Safeguard systems; one at Grand Forks Air Force Base, North Dakota, and another in Montana. Declared operational on October 1, 1975, the Grand Forks ABM system was closed down the next day by Congressional decree. Again, one of the main reasons for this was that there was little confidence that the system would actually work. Critics pointed out that Safeguard depended on a small number of large ground-fixed radar stations which themselves were vulnerable to attack. With the radars knocked out – there was nothing with which to defend them – the whole defence collapsed. No further attempts were made in the United States to install an ABM system and after the signing of the 1972 treaty, limiting the number of ABM interceptors to a mere 200, the use of anti-missile missiles was effectively dropped. In future, research was to concentrate on new wonder-weapons based on beam technology.

In the Soviet Union, work on ABM systems began in the 1960s. The first

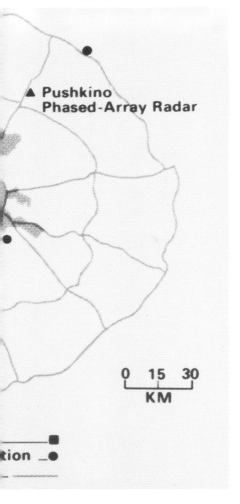

▲ **Pushkino Phased-Array Radar**

0   15   30
KM

ion

(ABM-1) system still stands today. Strung around the capital city of Moscow is a ring of four anti-ballistic missile bases, each equipped with nuclear-tipped missiles, known by their NATO code-name of Galosh. The Moscow system is, by all accounts, a modest affair. Within each of the four bases is housed 16 ageing, clumsy Galosh missiles with attendant tracking and radar guidance units. The system is alerted of an impending nuclear strike by a network of target-tracking radar stations (code-named 'Dog House' 'Cat House') positioned south of Moscow, and six Try Add 'guidance and engagement' radars. Each Galosh, if the attack came, would intercept its target above the atmosphere, before the warhead reached its terminal stage. It would kill its victim by bursting a thermonuclear warhead close to the target.

Like Sprint and Spartan, the Galosh ABM missile is armed with a nuclear warhead which destroys its target in one of three ways. First, by

Above: *A DOD artist's impression of the Soviet Galosh missile. First seen in the West in 1964, Galosh is comparable to Nike-Zeus.*

the emission of neutrons that penetrate almost any matter known to man. Piercing the heat shield and the outer protective jacket of the attacking ICBM, neutrons enter the fissile material itself causing it to melt and lose shape, rendering the missile useless.

The second way it can destroy its target is by the emission of X-rays which carry most of the energy released by the nuclear explosion. X-rays are highly effective above the atmosphere because they travel to their target without being absorbed by air molecules – and have the added advantage of not endangering people below. Their main disadvantage, as proved by the Johnston Island experiment of 1962, is that

Above: *Part of the modernization plans for the Moscow ABM system is the huge battle-management phased-array radar at Pushkino.*

exploding a nuclear weapon above the atmosphere releases huge amounts of EMP (electro-magnetic pulse). This has the counter-productive effect of destroying all ground radar and telecommunications systems: essential to any defence.

The third way of destroying a missile is by far the simplest: by the effect of blast. Blast, however, only operates in the atmosphere and attacking warheads can be shielded against it. Unless the defender also has a short-range defence in the shape of large numbers of very fast and very accurate missiles, armed with non-nuclear warheads, to intercept any warheads that escape the effects of blast, this method is the least satisfactory.

The nuclear-tipped ABM missile is a weapon of very doubtful value. Or so it was thought until Western Intelligence agents noted an up-dating and improving of the Galosh system in the early 1980s. Exactly what this up-

grading amounts to is still a matter of debate. But reports seem to suggest that the introduction of new 'phased array' radars — capable of tracking the skies in all directions, pinpointing multiple targets, and relaying their position to other stations in the system — centred at Pushkino radar station, a few miles outside Moscow, represents a new threat. This large, pyramid-shaped installation, 120ft (36.6m) high and 500ft (152.4m) wide at the base, will, when it is fully operational in the late 1980s, act as the centre for the defence of the Soviet capital. From Pushkino, information will be fed back to the six other phased radar sites located at Olenegorsk, Pechora, Sary Shagen

missile base, Lyaki — northern Moscow — Mishelevka and Krasnoyarsk. Together with Pushkino, these six sites are, some US Intelligence claim — despite strenuous Soviet denials — already in operation. According to Soviet sources these stations are nothing more than innocent satellite tracking stations, and are definitely not early-warning installations, banned by the 1972 ABM Treaty. While the placing of early-warning radar stations along a country's border is permitted by the treaty, placing them inland is not. This is because it is feared that such installations could be used for 'battle management' — tracking the course of incoming ICBMs and directing interceptors to destroy them.

Whether the sites really are phased radar stations or not, the Pentagon is certainly acting on the assumption that they are. From the Pentagon's point of view the events of the early 1980s were gloomy indeed. United States Intelligence revealed a number of developments which have helped fuel the demand in the US for an effective counter-ABM system. It is claimed that the Soviets are currently involved in an extensive modernization programme covering a wide range of anti-ballistic missile defences. Apart from the vastly improved radar facilities, now at their command, the lumbering Galosh missile is being replaced by the 'new' ABM-X-3 system by 1987. The system consists of the long-range SH-4 three-stage solid-fuel rocket armed with a sub-megaton neutron warhead designed to intercept RVs just outside the atmosphere, and the SH-4 short-range two-stage missile equipped with a small nuclear device for endo-atmospheric interception. The two missiles are technically, however, no more advanced than the US Spartan/Sprint system of the 1960s.

The threat too posed by the SA-10, once thought to be capable of an ABM role, is now known to have been exaggerated. The SA-10 is primarily aimed against cruise missiles and is roughly equivalent to the US Patriot. The missile that the Pentagon now fear is the SA-X-12. This truck-mounted, surface-to-air defence system is designed to counter high performance aircraft (such as the B1 bomber) and tactical ballistic missiles. Armed with a nuclear warhead the missile might also prove effective against SLBMs (known to their crews as 'slickums') which ring the Soviet Union and form a large part of the US nuclear deterrent. If the Soviets really have found an effective counter to them, then the Pentagon fear that the writing really is on the wall. Sceptics, however, remain unconvined that the system poses a serious challenge to a determined agressor.

One month after making the speech

which held the promise of "changing the course of human history", Ronald Reagan commissioned two teams of top scientists to prepare reports on how best to achieve this aim. The two teams – the Defensive Technologies Study Team (DTST) under Dr James C. Fletcher, an ex-director of NASA, and the Future Security Strategy Study (FSSS), headed by Fred C. Hoffman, director of Pan Heuristics (a Californian think tank) – met during the summer and early autumn of 1983 and, on October 1 they presented their findings to the President.

On the face of it, Fletcher's findings failed to endorse the President's hope that high-technology would provide

Below: *The quick-firing, truck-mounted surface-to-air SA-X-12 missile system (NATO code-named Gladiator) is capable of engaging high altitude aircraft and SLBMs.*

a total defensive shield, for the United States and her allies, against nuclear missile attack. Against the view expressed by Caspar Weinberger – "the defensive systems the President is talking about are not designed to be partial. What we want to try to get is a system which will develop a defense that is thoroughly reliable and total" – Fletcher said "total is one thing, substantial is another".

While a total defence of American cities (let alone those of her allies) was an idle dream, a more modest defence of major missile silos and centres of military communications, control and command was possible. "What you want is to minimize the casualties", Fletcher reported; but he warned that "There is no such thing as a nuclear umbrella".

To achieve this more modest defence Fletcher proposed a detailed time-table which, if adopted, would lead to the system being fully operational by the year 2000.

Phase 1 was the research stage. This would span a period of six years and cost an estimated $26 billion (£20.47 billion). Research would reveal the best space-based weapons system for destroying intercontinental

Below: *The USAF's Space Test Program satellite P-80-1 equipped with a laser optical communications receiver.*

Above: Shaped like an aircraft-carrier, Johnston Island was the test launch site for the ABM missile Sprint.

ballistic missiles. Stressing the need to improve and extend upon research already carried out, Fletcher suggested areas of research that might fruitfully fulfill the needs of the defensive system. These included chemical lasers, particle beam weapons, X-ray lasers, new, sophisticated orbiting optical spy equipment, and a 'surveilliance and battle management' space station, placed some 621,371 miles (100,000km) from Earth.

The technical challenge posed by such an enterprise was "great, but not insurmountable", and it was with a "sense of optimism", that Fletcher faced the future. At the close of this initial five-year period, Fletcher hoped that research would have reached the stage when it was possible for a future President (by 1990

Ronald Reagan will be 78) to decide whether to progress to phase 2 – the designing, building and testing of actual space weapons. Assuming that the decision to do this is made, partial deployment could begin. This, Fletcher suggests, might be coupled with a summit meeting with the Soviets aimed at drastically reducing each side's stockpile of nuclear warheads. The fourth and last phase would be the completion of the full deployment of the system matched with big reductions in the offensive missile forces of both sides. With such a defensive system, a first strike by the Soviets against the United States would, claimed Fletcher, have no military value.

The findings of the Future Security Strategy Study (FSSS), under Fred C. Hoffman, must have made even gloomier reading for the President. While endorsing the spending of money on research into ballistic missile defence, Hoffman warned against exaggerating the benefits of such a defence. Admitting that it could never be total, Hoffman added that even a limited "leakage" of the system – by which he meant a small number of warheads getting through to their target – would "destroy a very large part of our [US] urban structure and population". As an alternative to the defence of the civilian population, Hoffmann proposed a more limited defence of missile silos and "other military targets" (known as OMTs). Rather than replacing the notion of MAD – mutual assured destruction – as the President had promised in his speech, Hoffman believed Star Wars would actually strengthen it. Certainly, he held out little hope that a space-based ballistic missile defence would lead to MAS – mutual assured survival.

When James Fletcher's report was presented to the President, its proposals for a ballistic missile defence (BMD) held few surprises for scientists or defence specialists. Fletcher proposed a four-tier defensive system matching the four phases of an ICBM's flight from launch to destination – boost, post-boost, mid-course and terminal. Each stage of the defence, while offering opportunities for interception, presented its own difficulties and drawbacks. Each tier should aim at eliminating some 90 per cent of the attacking warheads, with an overall "leakage" – the

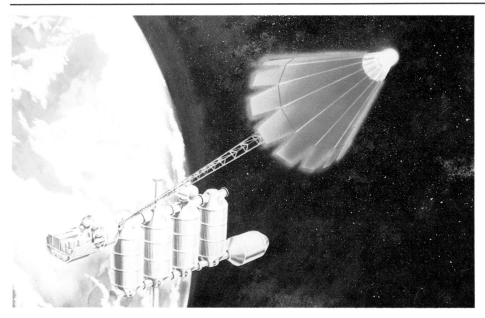

number of missiles getting through – of 0.1 per cent: a wildly optimistic figure according to the critics, and representing only three or four warheads actually hitting their targets.

But even the force of these few missiles would be destructive to a degree unseen in history. It has been calculated that if the "leakage" was one per cent, 80 per cent of American cities would be devastated. A five per cent leakage would result in the deaths of tens of millions of Americans, apart from the deaths that would occur later, due to fire, disease, and a breakdown of civil law and order. A five per cent hit rate by the attacking ICBMs would also, some scientists believe, be sufficient to trigger off a "nuclear winter".

Six months after the Fletcher report, Secretary of Defense Caspar Weinberger announced the setting up of the Strategic Defense Initiative Organization (SDIO), and the appointment of 51-year-old Air Force Lt. General James Abrahamson as its first director. The SDIO was charged with the task of translating the President's "vision of the future" and the recommendations of the Fletcher report into hard fact. Taking up his appointment on April 1, 1984, General Abrahamson set about the task with energy. "When I started I didn't know we had kinetic rail guns," he confided to reporters, "now we're firing them rather routinely". On the question of what, or who, SDI was intended to defend, he was vague. It was an issue which a year later remained vague.

In a profile published in the London

Above: *A Star Wars space-based nuclear-power fuelling station.*

Times of May 6, 1985, Abrahamson revealed some of the wonders SDI had already created – a computer the size of a child's building block capable of carrying out 40 million operations a second – but seemed uncertain about what SDI would achieve in the long run. Recognizing that "many people are afraid of the nuclear age", by the fact that there are children who say " 'well, maybe we will never grow up,' " – a feeling also expressed "in the way anti-nuclear protestors express their unwillingness to continue to live with this nuclear gun pointing at their heads", Abrahamson wished "to find a system whose primary purpose is to protect". "The purpose of the programme [SDI] is very clear," said Abrahamson. "It is to find a better way to preserve the peace, to avoid war".

For this reason he dislikes the phrase 'Star Wars'. It projects, he says, an "image of war-time purpose"; a purpose, he emphasized, that was a travesty of the truth. Nevertheless, he had to admit that the best one could hope from SDI was "as foolproof a system to defend ourselves against the single most dangerous weapon that man has produced, the nuclear ballistic missile".

The task then, of the Strategic Defense Initiative remains uncertain. While wishing to protect the whole population (children and anti-nuclear war protestors), it seems uncer-

tain whether a completely foolproof system is really possible. But anything less than a foolproof system would, as Fred C. Hoffmann predicted, result in the destruction of "a very large part of our [US] urban structure and population". The confused aims of SDI were evident even before it was officially launched in March 1984. While many members of the Reagan Administration – including the President himself – clung resolutely to the belief that the programme would protect *all* American citizens, those actually engaged in putting the

dream into practice, were motivated by much more modest aims.

Misgivings about Star Wars were also soon to be voiced privately by members of the NATO alliance. Rarely have such misgivings been expressed publicly. But in an uncharacteristically outspoken speech to the Royal United Services Institute in London in March 1985, the British Foreign Secretary, Sir Geoffrey Howe, stated that while he considered research into space-based ABM defence prudent – and Britain in December 1985 signed a deal to par-

ticipate commercially in Strategic Defense Initiative – Sir Geoffrey added the cautious warning that 'there would be no advantage in creating a new Maginot Line of the twenty-first century to be outflanked by relatively simpler and demonstrably cheaper countermeasures'.

In contrast to Sir Geoffrey Howe's conservative approach, General James Abrahamson's enthusiasm is typical of the new breed of America's 'spacemen'. His background, too, is typical: after flying 49 combat missions in Vietnam between 1964–65,

Above: *The electromagnetic rail gun uses electrical forces to shoot 'smart rocks' at ICBMs at a rate of 60 per second.*

he trained as an astronaut for the proposed Manned Orbiting Laboratory (a first attempt to produce a manned spacecraft), before the programme's cancellation in 1969. His subsequent rise to the top was relatively rapid. After two years' service as a member of the National Aeronautics and Space Council in the

European disquiet over the deployment of Pershing II, left, has extended to the fear that SDI will lead to an arms race in space. It has been the job of Star Wars supremo Lt. Gen. James A. Abrahamson, above, (ex-director of the F-16 fighter programme, right), to calm such fears.

White House, he progressed to become director of the F-16 Falcon fighter project before moving to head the Space Shuttle programme at NASA from 1981–1984; itself an indication of how deeply involved servicemen now are in NASA's activities. Described, rather unkindly, by some fellow servicemen as a 'SLOB' – "silver-lipped operator of bullshit" – it is commonly held that it was Abrahamson's honeyed tones that secured him the job. Like many men who now make up the USAF's new Space Command, Abrahamson sees himself as a pioneer of the 'new frontier'. For them the new mood in the White House and Pentagon ushered in by Ronald Reagan was good news. It seemed, at last, that their voice was not only being heard, but that it was being acted upon positively. Like Abraham-son, America's military spacemen believe – to borrow a term from *Star Wars* the movie – that 'The Force' is with them. With the advocates of SDI they share a vision of the twenty-first century in which America rules over a *Pax Americana,* policed by orbiting laser battle cruisers, in a way similar to the old notion of *Pax Britannica*

created by Britain's Royal Navy in the nineteenth century.

Today, the research programme launched to create a ballistic missile defence has achieved many of its objectives. Already, the map of the US economy has been drawn up on battle lines. "We have most of the industry in this country grouped one way or another into twenty teams," confided General Abrahamson to *Aviation Week* reporters in December 1984. "What we will be receiving is different opinions from various contractors where tradeoffs may be made."

The extent to which the economy of the United States is now involved in Star Wars research and development is shown on pages 54-55. The companies and contracts listed reflects the state of affairs at the beginning of 1985. Since then, even bigger contracts have been awarded to US companies already involved in major SDI projects. In the larger companies special SDI sections have been created to cope with the task of securing more of the SDI contracts. Among these are Lockheed (which manufactures Trident missiles); McDonnell Douglas (major cruise missile contractor); and Martin Marietta (leading Pershing missile manufacturer). In a booklet entitled *Strategic Defense: a Martin Marietta Commitment*, the company states that it is "prepared to contribute to the President's vision of a more stable world". Less altruistically, the company lists in an appendix those Congressional staff members worth "concentrating on", in order to secure SDI funding. Star Wars is big business, and the so-called "Beltway Bandits" — an industrialists' pressure group with offices on a Washington ring road — are hard at work on behalf of their clients.

"Money from heaven", is how one investment analyst described the multi-billion dollar bonanza. This vast investment — the biggest arms spending spree the world has ever seen — is being channelled into three main areas of research: tracking and surveillance systems; directed energy weapons; and kinetic energy weapons. How these three elements have shaped the Star Wars programme will be the subject of the next chapter.

MAJOR SDI CONTRACTORS (USA)

Company	Budget	Contract
Boeing Aerospace, Seattle, Washington.	$364,331 million	Airborne Optical System (AOS); Designating Optical Tracker (DOT); Booster Surveillance and Tracking System (BSTS); High-altitude Endo-atmospheric Defense System (HEDS); the Exo-atmospheric Re-entry Vehicle Interception System (ERIS) and various space-based laser components.
Lockheed Missiles & Space Co., Sunnyvale, California.	$240,165 million	Large Optics Demonstration Experiment (LODE); Homing Overlay Experiment (HOE); Laser-hardened, solid-propellent ballistic missile (an anti-SDI missile).
McDonnell Douglas Astronautics, Huntington Beach, California.	$236,802 million	Terminal Defense systems; HEDS.
LTV Corp. (Vought Corp) Fort Worth, Texas.	$210,989 million	Small Radar Interceptor Technology (SR Hit); anti-tactical ballistic missile. Also engaged in producing generators for the proposed electro-magnetic rail gun and ERIS.
Teledyne Brown Engineering Inc., Huntsville, Alabama.	$115,359 million	Contracted to develop various US Army SDI pro-grammes; also battle management computer software.
Aerojet General, Azuzu, California.	Over $50 million	Infrared sensors; BSTS; the Space Surveillance and Tracking System (SSTS).
Hughes Aerospace Group, Culver City, California.	$34,798 million	Optical & infrared sensors; laser & particle beam weapons; battle management systems.

Company	Budget	Contract
General Electric Co., Syracuse, New York.	Over $50 million	Space-based radar systems; Terminal Imaging Radar; electro-magnetic rail guns.
Honeywell Inc., Minneapolis, Minnesota.	Over $50 million	AOS computers; HOE; Advanced Warning System (AWS); infrared sensors.
Rockwell International, Seal Beach, California.	$88,744 million	Space-based laser (code-named ALPHA); Oxygen iodine chemical laser weapon; electro-magnetic rail gun; infrared sensors.
TRW, Redondo Beach, California.	$76,350 million	Booster Surveillance and Tracking System (BSTS), ALPHA chemical laser; missile vulnerability.
Grumman Aerospace, Bethpage, New York.	Over $20 million	Spaced-based radar antenna
ITEK Optical Systems, Lexington, Mass.	Over $20 million	Mirror for LODE
Martin Marietta Aerospace, Orlando, Florida.	Over $20 million	Kinetic energy weapons
RCA Government Systems Division, Moorestown, New Jersey.	Over $20 million	Alcor radar (used on the Kwajalein Atoll missile range); also radars that can detect Soviet missile penetration aids.
Westinghouse Electronics Corp., Research & Development Center, Pittsburgh, Pa.	Over $20 million	Electric discharge laser; particle beam weapons; electro-magnetic rail gun; also generators to power such guns.

CHAPTER 4

'TAKING THE TWINKLE OUT OF STARLIGHT'

George A. Keyworth II

"Before the President leaves office, we're going to be able
to demonstrate technology that convinces the Soviets
that we can – if we choose – develop a weapon to
shoot down their entire ICBM fleet as
it tries to enter space."

George A. Keyworth II, Scientific Advisor to President Reagan, June 4 1985

TO THE VISITOR IT looks like a rather scruffy oil refinery. Yet, on reflection, he would have to explain what an oil refinery was doing in the heart of the Santa Susana Mountains, not far from the sprawling conurbation of Los Angeles. In fact, according to Wayne Biddle of the *New York Times*, it is "the nearest thing to a Star Wars laser base anywhere in the Western world".

Run by the Rockwell International Corporation, this laser research unit has been in existence since 1976. With the coming of Star Wars the laboratory was given a new lease of life and a hefty chunk of the SDI budget. Work on high-energy lasers has come a long way since the days when Rockwell had to finance their own laser programme, code-named 'Rachel'. But the experience was useful, for, say Rockwell officials, 'Rachel' was a forerunner to Star Wars.

All over the United States, isolated, anonymous-looking office blocks today house some of the most ambitious and sophisticated scientific research that has ever been undertaken. Inside, men are working on projects that few outside know exist. They are the new breed of young,

clean-living, scientists, dedicated to the vision of a safe and happy United States protected by space-based wonder weapons; men like 42-year-old Lowell Wood, director of the 'O Group' at the Lawrence Livermore Weapons Research Laboratory in California. A protégé of Dr Edward Teller and a passionate supporter of the President's Star Wars programme, Wood is one of the principal brains behind the 'third generation' weapons programme – the first two generations having consisted of the atomic and the hydrogen bombs. Like many of the men who run these top secret weapons research laboratories, Wood believes that war with the Soviet Union is inevitable. "Someday," he is convinced, they will strike, "out of the clear blue sky, because that's the way they're postured, that's the way they're wired – BAM! ... It's chilling. It's hard to get out of your mind."

The conclusion for Wood and his colleagues is inescapable: America must do everything in its power to defeat a Soviet attack and ensure that at least some semblance of civilization survives. Like many in the White House, these men do not see that nuc-

lear war *need* be the end of everything. It is a conviction that shapes much of their work, and a belief without which much of what they do would be meaningless.

The coming of Star Wars has given substance to this feeling, and provided a framework for research that, until recently, was viewed, rather condescendingly, as 'interesting', if not a trifle esoteric. Today, all that has changed. Star Wars research and Star Wars projects are in the front line of American defence thinking. To a new generation of scientists, scholars, spacemen and old-fashioned anti-communists, Star Wars has provided a meaning, a coherence, that these disparate groups never before possessed. For the first time in over a generation, the dubious doctrine of MAD has been challenged by the more publicly appealing concept of Mutual Assured Survival – MAS.

Cutting through the millions of

Below: *Lawrence Livermore National Laboratory, California, centre for advanced SDI directed-energy weapons research.*

words written to describe, justify or condemn Star Wars, is a strategy that commands a measure of agreement among the programme's advocates. The blueprint is simple enough. "We would go after missiles in the boost phase, post-boost when the pentration aids had not yet been deployed," explains Lt. General Abrahamson. "And then high in the trajectory, as well as in the terminal area defenses, providing defense in depth".

Providing "defense in depth", consists in a four-tier structure (similar to Fletcher's recommendations), covering the four phases of an ICBM's flight. The aim, overall, is to destroy as many of the missiles or warheads at each of the four stages as possible, using a variety of space- and ground-based weapons. What George Keyworth calls, "taking the twinkle out of starlight".

How this four-tiered system works, and how recent research into 'third generation' weapons fits into this scheme is shown below. *Time,* in the chart, refers to the length of time available to each tier of the defence to destroy its targets.

Defence Tier	Time	Weapons
1. Boost Phase	3 minutes	Space-based chemical and excimer lasers; X-ray lasers; Particle beam weapons
2. Post-boost Phase	5 minutes	Kinetic energy weapons (KEW; also known as 'smart rocks'); Ground-based Free Electron Lasers (FEL); Space-based Directed Energy Weapons (DEW); Electro-magnetic Launchers (EML); 'Plasma Guns'
3. Mid-course Phase	20 minutes	Ground-based lasers; Air-launched Miniature Homing Vehicles (MHV — the F-15/Vought system currently developed as an ASAT weapon); KEW (such as the US Army's experimental HOW — Homing Overlay Experiment)
4. Terminal Phase	90 seconds	New, fast-accelerating, ground-based, anti-ballistic missiles of the Nike-Zeus/Nike-X type

BOOST PHASE DEFENCE

Phase 1 is the critical time. During the first three to five minutes that it takes an ICBM to rise above the Earth's atmosphere and reach near space, a missile is at its most vulnerable. The bright, fiery, plume given off by its rockets can easily be identified by infrared sensors based on orbiting satellites, and its course quickly calculated. It is also the critical time for the defence, for it is now that there is the best chance of knocking out a large percentage of the attacking missiles before they reach the post-boost stage when the MIRVs (Multiple Independently-targeted Re-entry Vehicles) and decoys separate. Once this happens, the defence could be presented with tens of thousands of warheads travelling in excess of 17,000 miles per hour (27,358km/h), together with perhaps an equal number of identical decoys.

If the defence cannot eliminate most of the attacking missiles during this first phase, then the defence, if it aims to be total, will have failed. This fact alone makes Star Wars different from all previous anti-ballistic missile systems. Sentinel, Safeguard and Sentry aimed at destroying the attacking warheads during their terminal phase as they re-entered the Earth's atmosphere, by which time they would have separated from the decoys which would have burned out on re-entry.

Finding a solution to the problem of how to locate, track, intercept and destroy an ICBM during its boost phase, lies at the heart of the Star Wars research programme. The task set is awesome indeed. To succeed, the system will have to invent, and have at its disposal, an entirely new range of weapons systems (directed-energy weapons and kinetic-energy weapons); a new system of automated control, command and communications of a complexity that no known computer or series of computers could cope with, and a new fleet of huge space transport vehicles of unprecedented power that have yet to leave the drawing board. And the whole system will have to work perfectly first time without ever having been properly tested. If a major malfunction were to occur, then the system, if it aimed at providing a total, or near total defence, would have failed.

In later sections of this chapter we look at the three main areas of Star Wars research, aimed at providing an adequate defence against an all-out Soviet land-based missile attack against the United States: Basing (see below); Weapons (pages 69-81); and Battle Management (pages 81-85). Each of these three areas of research aims at solving the problem of locating, tracking, intercepting and destroying Soviet ICBMs in each phase of the four-phased flight of an ICBM (boost, post-boost, mid-course and terminal). But as we shall see in Chapter 5, even if such a system were to be deployed, it would still leave the United States vulnerable to other forms of Soviet nuclear attack.

Basing

To strike at Soviet ICBMs in their boost, post-boost and mid-course phases prohibits the use of ground-based weapons unless those weapons were in some way linked to a space-based system. No weapon based in the United States, unless linked to a space system, could intercept and destroy an ICBM launched from a land-based silo, deep in the Soviet Union. Ground-based lasers cannot fire a beam around the curve of the Earth. To hit a missile above the Soviet Union, the laser weapon would have to be based either on a fleet of orbiting battle stations, or linked to a space-based system. Currently, there are two ground- and space-based linked systems under consideration. One involves placing mirrors in space to bounce laser beams fired from Earth on to the target; the other, the so-called 'pop-up' system, envisages placing the laser apparatus on a rocket which, when it reaches a certain height in space, would be able to 'see' the target over the horizon. Each system has its advantages and drawbacks, and each has its advocates and detractors in the battle of words waged for the rich SDI contracts. In the final analysis, politics could well prove to be as decisive a factor in the choice of system as the physics.

Orbiting Laser Battle Stations

This scheme has perhaps attracted more enthusiasm among SDI advocates than any other proposal currently under review. In theory, the idea is simple enough. It involves placing a number of satellites armed with laser weapons in low orbit to guard against a possible Soviet nuclear missile attack. Since lasers deliver energy at the speed of light, 186,000 miles per second (300,000 km/sec) – not surprising since lasers *are* light – a laser weapon based on an orbiting satellite could easily, in theory, shoot down any of the present generation of Soviet ICBMs before they reached their post-boost phase and unpacked their MIRVs (Multi-Independently targeted Re-entry Vehicles). But the scheme soon runs into difficulties when looked at a little more closely.

Satellites – and the laser battle station is essentially an armed satellite – in low orbit would pass over the Soviet Union only twice in every 24 hours. To ensure continuous coverage of Soviet silos would require a fleet of laser battle stations placed in permanent orbit. Estimates of the number needed varies from a low 90, to a high 2,400, each one needing at least a shuttle-full of fuel to fire their lasers.

Below: *A laser beam fired from USAF facility at Maui, Hawaii, streaks across the night sky in an October 1985 SDI test.*

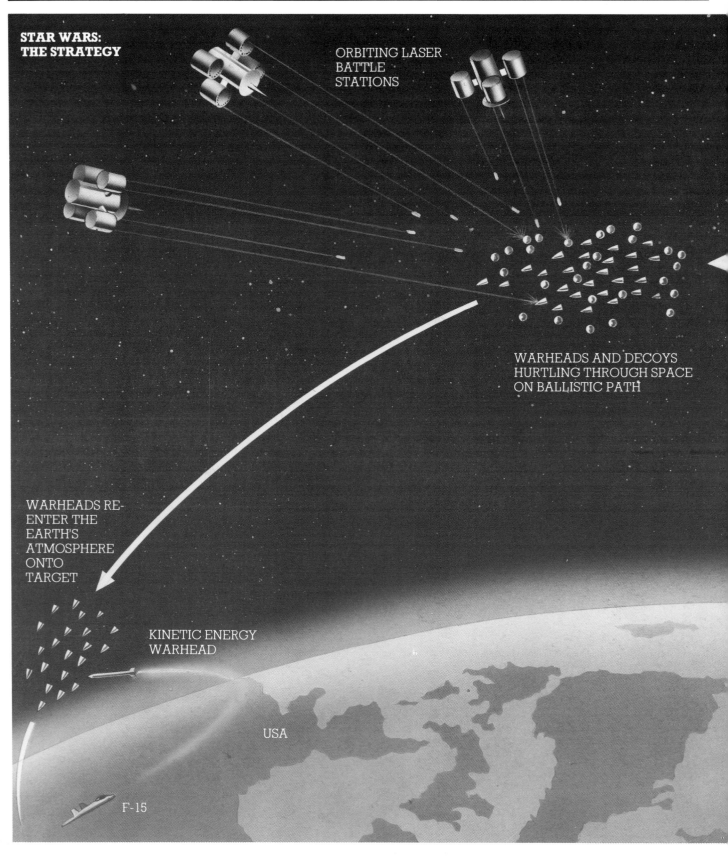

STAR WARS: THE STRATEGY

ORBITING LASER BATTLE STATIONS

WARHEADS AND DECOYS HURTLING THROUGH SPACE ON BALLISTIC PATH

WARHEADS RE-ENTER THE EARTH'S ATMOSPHERE ONTO TARGET

KINETIC ENERGY WARHEAD

USA

F-15

6 Having waited 30 minutes, terminal defence has now only seconds to identify, track and destroy what is left of the attack. KE weapons (F-15 ASAT-type) and ABM missiles are launched to avert Armageddon.

5. As the thinning cloud of projectiles re-enters the atmosphere, decoys and penetration aids disintegrate and the remaining warheads shreik Earthwards at over 14,000mph.

4 Warheads, decoys and penetration aids now follow a ballistic trajectory through space. Twenty minutes from target, the defence must correctly identify the real warheads and destroy them.

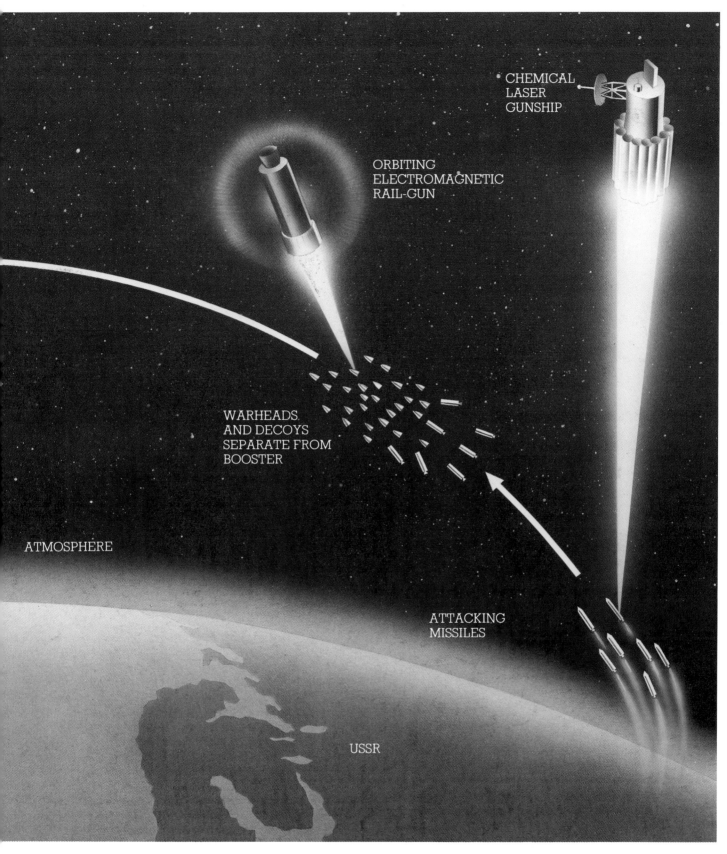

CHEMICAL
LASER
GUNSHIP

ORBITING
ELECTROMAGNETIC
RAIL-GUN

WARHEADS
AND DECOYS
SEPARATE FROM
BOOSTER

ATMOSPHERE

ATTACKING
MISSILES

USSR

3. Five minutes after launch, the warheads, decoys and penetration aids separate. If this phase is reached with most of the attack still intact, then the defence has failed.

2. Before the post-boost phase (five minutes) when thousands of warheads and decoys separate, laser gunships and electromagnetic railguns would have to destroy most missiles within minutes of launch.

1. The boost phase is when an ICBM is at its most vulnerable and when a space-based defence has the best chance of defeating the attack. Early warning satellites alert the defence of an attack.

*Above: Based in space, giant mirrors
will direct laser beams fired from
Earth on to the attacking missiles.*

Apart from the cost of building, arming, fuelling and transporting such stations into space, the reaction of the Soviet government to the deployment of such a system, must also be taken into consideration. There can be little doubt in the minds of America's military planners that the Soviets would react very strongly indeed to any attempt by the United States to place a fleet of armed satellites over the skies of the Soviet Union. One has only to consider what the reaction of the United States itself would be were the Soviets to place a similar system over the United States. It could well provoke the very attack the system was designed to prevent.

What steps the Soviets might take, and what counter-measures they could adopt in the event of SDI being deployed, will be looked at in Chapter 5. If SDI were ever to be deployed, it could spark off a chain of action and reaction which would know no bounds. If the system was deployed, then the United States, for example,

would also have to deploy another system to defend its space-based assets against attack. And the Soviets, no doubt, would soon obtain the means of outfoxing that defence. So the US would be called upon to defeat the Soviet counter-attack. And so on, and so on. But, as many experts have pointed out, the advantage will probably always lie with the aggressor, since it will always be cheaper to outfox, outmanoeuvre and overwhelm the defence than for the defence to defeat the attack. For the star warriors, such a scenario must make gloomy reading.

Ground-based Lasers

This system avoids basing a fleet of orbiting battle stations in space by stationing excimer laser weapon bases (see pages 71-72) on the tops of mountains on Earth. Fired, the laser beams would be directed on to 5 metre relay mirrors placed either in geosynchronous orbit (24,000 miles [36,000 km] from Earth), or semi-syn-

chronous orbit (10,000 miles [17,000 km] from Earth), and then bounced back on to 'fighting mirrors' in low orbit. These 'fighting mirrors' would be equipped with powerful infra-red telescopes (to pick up the ascending rocket's give-away infra-red plume emitted from its engines) which would lock on to the ascending booster rockets and direct the laser beam on to the target.

The idea of bouncing a laser beam fired from Earth on to an orbiting mirror thousands of miles in space, then bouncing it back again, though considered by some to be a preposterous idea, has, in fact, already been shown to work – at least on a small scale. On Monday, June 17, 1985, at 7.33am, local time, the 2,000-ton US space shuttle *Discovery* rose above the low scrubland of Cape Canaveral. Onboard were five American astronauts (including Shannon Lucid, a lady scientist born in Shanghai), together with a Saudi Arabian prince (Sultan ibn Salman ibn Abdulaziz), and a 39-year-old French Air Force Colonel, Patrick Baudry, who was to study the effects of weightlessness on the human cardiovascular and nervous systems. While interest centred for much of the world's press on the tricky problem facing Prince Sultan of how to locate Mecca while travelling at 12,000mph (19,200km/h) – to observe Islamic law which requires him to pray five times a day facing the holy city – the enterprise was historic for another reason. Code-named 'Mission 51-C', the shuttle was to conduct an experiment – the High-Precision Tracking Experiment – to test the ability of a ground-based laser beam deflector to accurately track an object in near-Earth orbit.

The first attempt ended in failure. Instead of feeding the computers onboard *Discovery* with instructions in feet, someone at ground control issued them in nautical miles. Then there were winds of 80mph (128km/h) to contend with. But just before dawn on Friday, June 21, to the sound, rather inappropriately, of Russian composer Piotr Tchaikovsky's *1812 Overture*, a brilliant bluish-green beam flashed from the top of Mount Haleakala, a 10,000ft (3,048m) peak on the tiny island of Maui, Hawaii, streaked 220 miles (354km) through space and hit a 'retroreflector' mirror the size of a dinner plate mounted on the port side of *Discovery*. The beam locked on to the 8in (20.3cm) reflector for several seconds before bounding back to Earth.

It was, from all accounts, a spectacular success. For Lt. General James A. Abrahamson, the experiment seemed to justify his optimism and to confound the critics. Smarting from the failure of the first attempt – viewed by the Pentagon as crucial – Abrahamson had reacted strongly. "These people," he said, "are seizing on ridiculous things to try to criticize the [SDI] program. They either have an axe to grind or don't understand how experiments are conducted. If your car doesn't start in the morning, does that mean 'star wars' isn't going to work? There's no logic in it" – a rebuke aimed at John Pike, head of space policy for the Washington-based Federation of American Scien-

tists. After the first, bungled, attempt, Pike had facetiously observed, "if they can't do a simple experiment like this, what are they going to do in combat? You can't reschedule World War III. Are they going to ask the Russians to come back?"

But despite the public pleasure expressed by the star warriors at the success of the second experiment, there were still some awkward questions being asked. If the system was open to simple human error, what confidence could anyone have in it defeating an all-out nuclear attack?

Revelations made public after the return of the space shuttle *Discovery* to Earth, did little to allay such fears. Receiving the wrong instructions, the shuttle turned itself a full 180 degrees so that when the first laser beam struck, the shuttle was facing the wrong way. A matter of small concern perhaps in an experiment, but potentially disastrous when trying to track the course of thousands of

warheads during a real attack.

Ground-based lasers themselves suffer from a number of defects and difficulties. Weather and cloud can affect a laser's performance. Turbulence in the atmosphere produces distortions in the beam. One way of overcoming this may be to base an additional laser weapon closer to the 'fighting mirror', to act as a kind of 'booster' to the main laser. Another possible solution is to programme the controlling computers to interpret the varying weather conditions so that they can adjust the strength of the beam accordingly.

To produce a laser beam powerful enough to pass through the Earth's atmosphere would require between

Below: *This vivid display of colour is what was seen by members of the space shuttle 'Discovery' when a laser beam was fired at it from Maui, Hawaii on 21 June, 1985.*

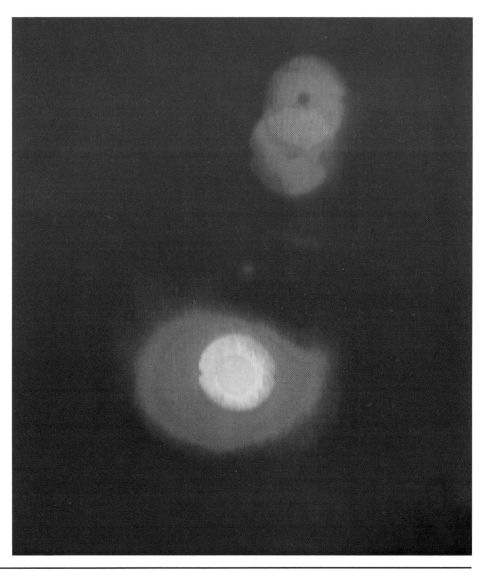

100 and 300 megawatts (a million kilowatts) of electricity – the equivalent of between 20 and 60 per cent of current US domestic electrical output. Obviously, there is no way in which electricity from the US national grid could suddenly be switched to a series of laser battle stations at a moment's notice. Though the electricity could be created by specially constructed power stations, the cost of such an endeavour would run into hundreds of billions of dollars: a sum that would be burned up in seconds should the system ever be used.

'Pop-up' system

This is by far the simplest and cheapest method of overcoming the curvature of the Earth in order to direct a laser beam on to an ICBM during its boost phase. The system works by launching a nuclear device into space and directing the X-ray laser beams, generated by the explosion, along rods projecting from the device on to the attacking missiles. To work efficiently, the system has just a microsecond before it is itself consumed in a fireball.

To launch such a device from the United States would be fruitless because the 'pop-up' booster would have to accelerate many times faster than the attacking missile if it were to fire its weapon and intercept the target before it had completed its boost phase. To remedy this, an X-ray laser weapon could be launched from submarines placed as close as possible to Soviet missile silos. Located in the Arabian Sea, the Norwegian Sea or the northern Indian Ocean, the interceptor would thus be separated from the Soviet missile silos by a distance of some 2,485 miles (4,000km). The interceptor would have to soar to a height of some 584 miles (940km) before it could 'see' an ICBM at an altitude of some 124 miles (200km).

In theory, the interceptor would reach its target, a Soviet ICBM comparable to the current US MX missile type, in 120 seconds. But it would be impossible for such a 'pop-up' weapon to engage a large number of Soviet missiles, because many silos are located more than 2,485 miles (4,000km) away, and the submarines could not launch all their missiles simultaneously. And there is a more fundamental weakness to the system. X-ray lasers cannot be used in the lower atmosphere. If the Soviets were to build ICBMs with a much-shortened boost phase, then X-ray lasers would be ineffective.

In an article published in *Scientific American* (October 1984), Professor Hans Bethe (one of the founding fathers of America's nuclear weapons programme and a Nobel physics prize winner) claims that ". . . all pop-up interception schemes, no matter what kind of anti-missile weapon they employ, depend on the assumption that the USSR will not build ICBMs with a boost phase so short that no pop-up system could view the burning booster". As the Fletcher enquiry itself reported, it is perfectly possible to devise a missile with a boost phase of only 60 seconds or less, with the loss of only 20 per cent of its payload. If the Soviets were to do that, then whatever pop-up system the Americans were to deploy would, on present reckoning, be doomed to failure.

To destroy an ICBM attack during the boost phase, the first tier of the system will have to be fully automated. The launching of an attack could only be detected by infra-red sensors mounted on surveillance satellites. These warning signals would have to be sent to and interpreted by the laser battle stations which would then have to locate and track the target, direct the weapon system on to the moving target, record whether a hit had been made (if it missed then that information would have to be passed on to the second tier of the defence for it to intercept the warhead), then switch to another of the possible 10,000 or more targets. And the system must complete these complex operations within some 60 seconds. If the system, at present, fails to direct a single laser beam on to a single target, at a prearranged time and location, critics see little hope of it taking on the entire Soviet fleet within the foreseeable future.

Not everyone agrees with this pessimistic point of view, of course. According to Professor Hans Berliner, a computer expert at the Carnegie-Mellon University, Pittsburgh, "The technology is do-able. Two hundred years from now, the Star Wars control problem may be child's play." And to back up his claim, Professor Berliner points to the super, chess-playing computer he has built, capable of working out 175,000 moves a second.

"POP-UP" SYSTEM

"POP-UP" SYSTEM

Nevertheless, no one doubts the complexity of devising a fully automated computer control system, capable of coping with over 10 million instructions, without a serious error being committed. It would take a leap in the science of artificial intelligence (which is still in its infancy) to produce such a machine, and few can see that happening in the immediate future.

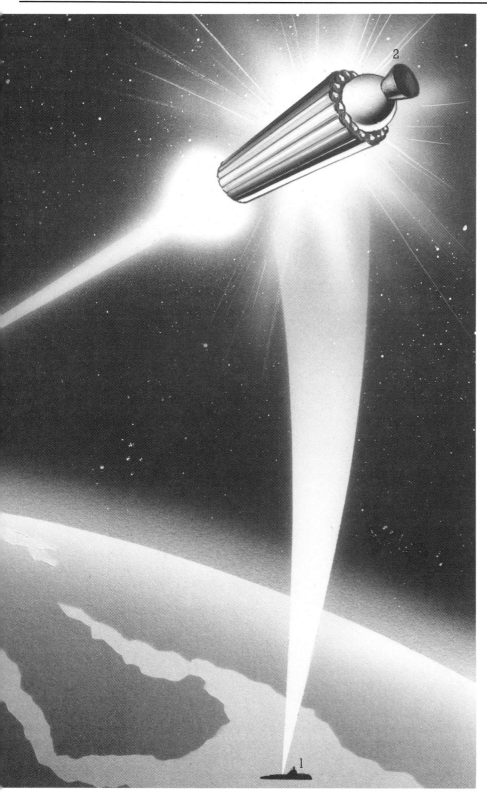

flight, the MIRV or 'bus' (as it is commonly called) continues to ascend before releasing its cargo of warheads, decoys and penetration aids. This complex manoeuvring operation takes some five minutes, once the initial, boost phase has been completed. To achieve a high kill rate, the defence will have to intercept and destroy as many of these surviving 'buses' before they unpack their deadly cargo. The advantage the defence has during this phase is that, if the first phase has achieved a high success rate, there should be few targets to aim at. Once the buses have unpacked their cargo, however, the defence is presented with many thousands of targets, both real warheads and decoys.

Detecting the bus's presence, however, is not nearly as simple as detecting the missile in its boost phase. The bus's manoeuvring engines are much smaller and they give off a much smaller infra-red 'signature' for the defence's sensors to pick up.

In addition to lasers and particle beam weapons, kinetic energy weapons could also be used at this stage. These weapons (examined in more detail, pages 76-79) consist of rockets, homing vehicles, or simply metal pellets fired at the attacking bus, destroying their target by impact. The most celebrated weapon of this arsenal is the electromagnetic rail gun (see pages 79-81). Kinetic energy weapons are also known as 'smart rocks'. Their main disadvantages are their limited range, measured in hundreds, rather than thousands of miles, their slow speed – a maximum of 25 miles per second – and the fact that they can operate only at high altitudes. But unlike the more fancy lasers and particle beam weapons, kinetic energy weapons actually exist, have been tested, and are known to work.

MID-COURSE PHASE DEFENCE
Once the warheads (and decoys) reach the mid-course phase they follow a ballistic trajectory (see diagram pp. 60-61) which lasts about 20 minutes. If the defence has failed to eliminate most of the missiles and buses in the first two phases, then the third line of defence faces an almost impossible task. Most Soviet ICBMs carry ten warheads each — a number limited by treaty. But they could carry as many as 30 warheads, in addition to

POST-BOOST PHASE DEFENCE
All three methods of basing a first tier defence against ICBMs can also be used in the second phase defence. The defence could also, conceivably, use more than one weapons system at any one time. Chemical lasers (see pages 70-71), particle beam weapons and X-ray lasers might all be used in conjunction, fired from

Fired from a US submarine (1), an X-ray laser would direct X-radiation (2) by nuclear explosion on to the attacking ICBM (3) in the microsecond before destruction.

ground-based stations, orbiting battle stations, or from submarines.

In the second phase of the ICBM's

numerous decoys and other 'penetration aids' (balloons, chaff – radar-reflecting wire – and infra-red-emitting aerosols simulating the 'signature' of warheads) to confuse the defence (see Countermeasures, Chapter 5).

The defence has the task of either eliminating *all* targets, or picking out the real warheads from the thousands of moving objects all travelling through space at the same velocity. Since it is unlikely that any system could ever afford to field the

number of weapons needed to intercept all targets in the 'threat cloud' individually (calculated by the US Union of Concerned Scientists to be some 70,000 in order to achieve a kill rate of 99.9 per cent against 10,000 targets), some means of discriminating between warheads and decoys will have to be found.

Proposals range from sophisticated sensors (perhaps lasers) able to locate and examine each object in turn, to the sledge-hammer approach which might involve the detonation of

Above: *In the terminal phase of an ICBM's flight RVs streak towards their target. If SDI works few will get through, but enough, say critics, to ensure Armageddon.*

nuclear bombs close to the threat cloud in the hope of sweeping away the lighter decoys. A more subtle approach, and one that is certain to prove to be more efficient, is the US Army's kinetic-energy weapon, code-named HOE – Homing Overlay

Experiment (see pages 77-78 for details). This weapon, already successfully tested, has illustrated that it is possible for an interceptor missile to seek out and destroy a nuclear warhead travelling through space at a speed of 22,000mph (35,405km/h). The test, conducted over the Pacific Ocean on June 10, 1984, proved that it was possible to 'hit a bullet with a bullet' – something SDI critics had always said was impossible. But however sophisticated or crude the defence might be in locating and de-

stroying targets, it might always be cheaper for the offense to throw up more targets than for the defence to shoot them down.

One important advantage midcourse defence does have, however, over the boost and post-boost phase, is the time available in which to locate, track, intercept and destroy targets. Lasers, particle beam weapons and kinetic energy weapons would again be deployed. But they would have a greater chance of defeating the attack if they could

Above: *US Army's HOE homing and kill vehicle. As the vehicle homes in on an incoming warhead a sensor releases the 15ft metal umbrella destroying the target by impact.*

identify and isolate their real targets – a task considerably more difficult than during the boost and post-boost phases when the rockets and buses emit strong infra-red radiation. Midcourse, the warheads give out only faint signals, difficult to pick up.

TERMINAL PHASE DEFENCE

Streaking back into the Earth's atmosphere at an altitude of between 60-90 miles (97-145km), those re-entry vehicles (RVs) and decoys that had managed to elude the third defence tier would soon separate, with the lighter decoys and penetration aids burning up (by the action of friction in the atmosphere), and falling away. The remaining warheads and heavy decoys would then glow, before turning white-hot and hurtling Earthwards at a velocity of 4 miles per second (14,400mph, 23,174km/h), towards Armageddon.

Technically, terminal defence is the simplest tier of defence to devise. The targets are clearly identifiable and can be picked up and tracked by ground-based sensors and radar. But there is little chance of protecting civilian targets at this stage. Most of the warheads targeted on people and property will be 'salvage-fused', that is, they detonate if intercepted in the upper atmosphere, causing as much, if not more damage than if they had struck the target on the ground. If the defence aims at protecting hardened missile silos, able to withstand a one-megaton detonation at only 100yd (91m), then it stands a better chance. But to destroy successfully the remaining warheads in the atmosphere, the system will have, at most, 90 seconds.

The range of weapons at the disposal of such a defence is impressive: fast-accelerating interceptor missiles that destroy their target on impact; the Vought/F-15/ASAT air-launched miniature homing vehicle; 'smart rocks' that home in on the RVs destroying them on impact; and lasers capable of operating in the upper atmosphere. But whatever weapon was used to intercept the unstoppable warheads, they must travel at the same speeds as those of the warheads themselves. They would also have a very limited range, which would mean that vast numbers of weapons would be needed in order to provide an effective defence. According to Professor Aston B. Carter of Harvard University, in order to stop the re-entry vehicles surviving from an initial launch of 1,400 Soviet ICBMs, the United States would have to field a fleet of some 280,000 interceptors.

Below: *The US Navy's high-energy laser test site, San Juan, Capistrano, California. In 1977 a prototype laser device was fired against a tethered Huey helicopter.*

STAR WARS: THE WEAPONS

Lasers

The word 'laser' is an acronym for Light Amplification by Stimulated Emission of Radiation. The first use of the laser was demonstrated in 1960 and its potential as a weapon soon realized. Though over 2 billion dollars were spent in the United States during the 1960s and '70s to develop a laser weapon, no practical, operational laser weapon has yet been produced. Indeed, it may be some twenty years before even a prototype laser weapon may be ready for testing in space. Reports, circulated by the CIA (and said to be believed by US Secretary of Defense, Caspar Weinberger) that the Russians already possess an operational ground-based laser gun capable of shooting down US satellites, is dismissed by informed experts as fantasy. For the Soviets to have developed so sophisticated a weapon when US scientists, helped by huge financial and technical ad-

vantages, have yet to build one themselves, seems most unlikely.

The reason why lasers are such prized weapons is because they travel at a speed of 186,000 miles per second (300,000km/sec) – the speed of light. Laser beams *are* light, but unlike the light produced by an ordinary domestic light bulb, the light from a laser is almost perfectly parallel and of a single wavelength. The light from a domestic light bulb, by contrast, is fuzzy, of unequal wavelength and thrown out in all directions. The energy from a laser, therefore, is remarkably pure and powerful. Based in space, a laser beam can cover hundreds of thousands of miles in a fraction of a second to burn a hole in the outer skin of an ICBM, playing havoc with the missile's guidance system and rendering its nuclear warheads impotent. Lasers make ideal weapons because they give no warning. Their existence is known only when they strike. Perfectly aimed, there is little the target can do to avoid destruc-

Above: *Using electromagnets, subatomic particles are accelerated at the Lawrence Livermore Laboratory to speeds approaching that of light.*

tion. "People have a hard time accepting the idea that lasers can kill at a distance," says Louis Marquet, who heads directed-energy research for the SDI Organization, "but we now have the ability to burn holes in chunks of steel at a very great distance," – though scientists in the United States are hedging their bets by experimenting with ways of protecting US ICBMs against possible Soviet laser attack.

The term 'laser' has been used (and is often used) as if there was just one 'laser' weapon. This is not so. Currently, research in the United States (and the Soviet Union, even on a modest scale in Britain), is being conducted into many different types of laser weapons. Broadly, these fall into three main categories:

1. **Chemical Lasers**

2. **Excimer Lasers**

3. **X-ray Lasers**

Chemical Lasers

These are the most powerful lasers now in use. They are produced by utilizing the reaction between two gases, such as hydrogen and fluorine. At the US High Energy Laser Test Range in New Mexico, a 2.2 megawatt device known by its apt acronym MIRACL (Mid-Infra-Red Advanced Chemical Laser) has already been tested. But to kill an ICBM in space would require a device at least ten times as powerful. And MIRACL is not yet even classified as a prototype weapon: that may be years ahead. To operate as a ground-based weapon, it must overcome the problem of the atmosphere which, as we have seen, can play havoc with the power and purity of a laser beam. One way of overcoming this problem is to place the laser weapon onboard an aircraft. In a series of tests carried out in the late 1970s and early 1980s, the USAF did just this. Placing a 400 kilowatt carbon-dioxide laser weapon onboard a converted Boeing 707, renamed the Airborne Laser Laboratory (ALL), they tested the feasibility of using a laser weapon in the upper atmosphere against a missile.

In early February 1981 the weapon was used against an air-launched AIM-9L Sidewinder air-to-air missile. Though the beam hit the target, it did not destroy it. Two days later, a second attempt was made, also against an AIM-9L Sidewinder. Again the laser intercepted the target, this time locking on to it for several seconds. (Because a chemical laser's wavelength has a tendency to spread out, it has to be held precisely on the same spot on a missile's skin for perhaps as long as seven seconds in order to penetrate it. During that time, the missile would have risen at least a further 20 miles.)

In July 1983 a further series of ALL tests was carried out against five Sidewinder missiles, in which the laser weapon managed to change the missiles' course. Other tests entailed the shooting down of sea-skimming cruise-missile drones over the Pacific Ocean.

The US Navy also has its laser weapon programme, which began in the 1970s under the code-name Sea Lite. Tests were carried out from the autumn of 1977 using a 400kW weapon against a variety of targets, including TOW wire-guided anti-tank missiles, and at the Navy's test site at San Juan, Capistrano, California, against tethered Huey helicopters. The ultimate aim of the project was to produce a 2.2 megawatt laser powerful enough to be used as an operational weapon. Cancelled in 1983, the Sea Lite programme has now been incorporated into a DARPA (Defense Advance Research Project Agency) programme, code-named Skylight. In the opinion of an Administration spokesman, Sea Lite "could be used in tests for a gee whiz experiment, but it would not provide a basic military capability".

But by far the most ambitious chemical laser research is being conducted under another DARPA programme, called Triad. Triad consists of three main elements: *Alpha,* which aims at creating a 5 megawatt hydrogen-fluoride, high-energy laser capable, according to Department of Defense officials, of being scaled up to provide 25 megawatts; *LODE* (Large Optics Demonstration Experiment) – a 4 metre mirror to aim and focus the Alpha laser beam on to a moving target; and *Talon Gold,* the production of target-acquisition, tracking, and precision-pointing equipment necessary for the finding, tracking and interception of an ICBM.

As an effective weapon against ICBMs, however, chemical lasers have a very limited use and capability. The power presently being produced by the most sophisticated chemical lasers (a 2 megawatt device is planned on being tested in 1987), is

This limitation was spelled out in James Fletcher's report to President Reagan in October 1983, when he recommended that although chemical laser research should continue (though less money should in future be apportioned to it than previously planned), research into more fruitful weapons, such as excimer lasers and X-ray lasers should be pursued more vigorously.

Though chemical lasers may have fallen out of favour as ICBM-killers, they are increasingly being touted as potential satellite slayers. This new-found role is reflected, for example, by the USAF awarding TRW and Rocketdyne fat contracts to develop an oxygen-iodine chemical laser with an ASAT capability. According to DARPA director Robert Cooper, the United States will, by the mid-1990s, have developed the means of shooting down 'hostile' satellites by chemical laser battle stations orbiting in space. Clearly, the distinction between 'defensive' and 'offensive' space weapons is becoming increasingly fuzzy. What can be used as a defence against ballistic missiles, may also be used for offensive purposes against space assets. Such a view, most forcibly expressed by Dr Rather, Vice-President of Kaman Aerospace Corporation – "a system of space battle stations designed to stop nuclear attack, also may have the potential to attack selected targets in space, in the atmosphere, or down on the surface of the Earth" – is vehemently denied by SDI advocates. Dr Edward Teller, among others, states "unequivocally, that the technology being researched is defensive and not offensive". It is a controversy in which means and motives have obviously become confused.

Excimer Lasers

These lasers are created by the reaction of two types of gas, typically fluorine and argon or xenon, stimulated by electrical power to produce pulses of beams of high energy in a fraction of a second. They make ideal

Above: *The USAF's Airborne Laser Laboratory (ALL) – a converted Boeing 707 fitted with a high-energy chemical laser in the turret.*

Below: *Code-named Talon Gold, the USAF and DARPA will test a laser pointing and target-tracking device on the space shuttle in the late 1980s.*

puny compared to the mighty 25 megawatt lasers spoken of by SDI officials. To destroy the Soviet Union's ICBM fleet of 1,400 land-based missiles would, it has been calculated, require 300 25-megawatt hydrogen-fluoride laser battle stations in low orbit, each equipped with 10m optically perfect mirrors. If such a system were to produce a 1,864 mile (3,000km) 'kill radius', then it could, according to experts, in the absence of any countermeasures, destroy an all-out Soviet nuclear missile attack. Clearly, the chemical lasers currently being produced have a long way to go to meet this challenge.

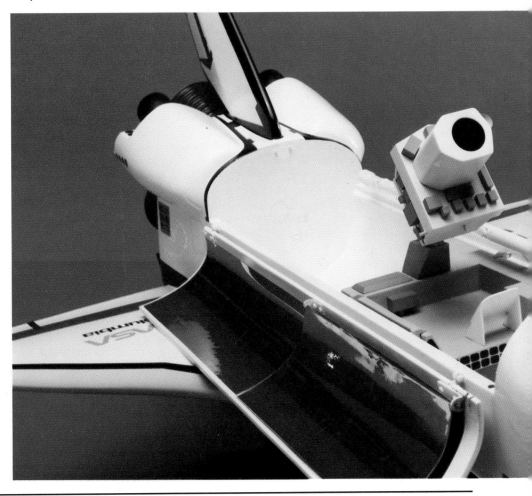

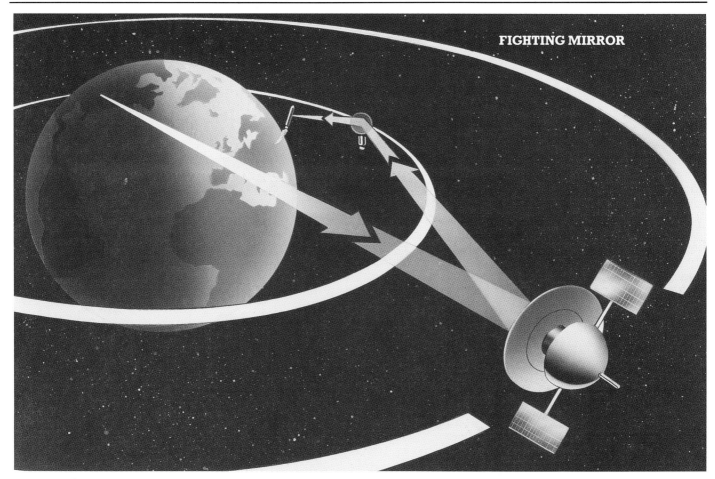

FIGHTING MIRROR

anti-missile weapons because they can destroy their target by concentrating on it for just a second or more. But they suffer one major drawback as a space-based weapon: they require laser generating equipment which is bulky in the extreme. Indeed, there is no known way of placing such apparatus in space. Consequently, excimer laser battle stations would have to be placed on the tops of mountains on Earth. Even here, however, they encounter problems. Their beams, if shot straight into space, would suffer from the same phenomenon that causes stars to appear to twinkle in the night sky. To solve this problem, scientists have suggested that excimer lasers should be fired at huge reflecting mirrors placed in geostationary orbit. Such mirrors would perform the dual function of 'de-twinkling' the beams (making them concentrated and pure) and bouncing them back on to a series of 'fighting mirrors' placed in low orbit (as we have seen).

How big these mirrors need to be is a matter of debate, with estimates varying accordingly. Some say 20ft (7m) mirrors would suffice, while others maintain that 90ft (27m) may

prove to be too small. But whatever the true figure (no one really knows), all are agreed that such mirrors would need to be optically perfect. The slightest scratch or warping would result in the scattering of any beam fired. (Mirrors placed on top of chemical laser battle stations to direct the beam on to the target would suffer from the same problems, but the size of mirror required is a mere 30ft [9m].) And the mirrors would not only have to be perfect, they would also have to be robust enough to withstand the massive amounts of laser power directed at them and the rigours of being launched into orbit.

The accuracy of aim required by such mirrors is staggering. Across thousands of miles of empty space the laser beams would have to be directed on to the attacking missiles (in the boost phase) to within a few feet, then held on to the target for several seconds for the laser to do its work while the missile is still moving. Nor is this all. Detecting a booster rocket is fairly easy, because of the distinctive bright, hot glow (infra-red radiation) given off by the rocket's engines. But some system would have to be invented to direct the laser not

Fired from the ground, an excimer laser is aimed at a giant mirror in geosynchronous orbit. The beam is bounced back to a smaller 'fighting mirror' which reflects the beam on to the rising booster.

only at the fiery plume, but on to the body of the missile itself. And to do that, say the experts, will require not only new radars of an incredible sensitivity (possibly laser radar), but also yet another set of mirrors (the so-called 'fighting mirror') of equal optical perfection, but ten times the diameter of the laser mirror itself — because infra-red radiation has longer wavelengths than excimer laser wavelengths.

Not surprisingly, there is a growing body of opinion that is actively urging the SDI Organization to look again at the idea that first commended itself to President Reagan: the X-ray laser.

X-ray Lasers
It was, it will be recalled, this device (brainchild of Dr Edward Teller) that first fired President Reagan's imagination and helped formulate the whole idea of a space-based 'strategic

defence'. More recently, the significance of the X-ray laser as a component of the Star Wars system has been carefully, and repeatedly, played down by Administration officials. Such subterfuge is hardly surprising. To station a nuclear device in space (and some proposals recommend the placing of some 1,400 orbiting H-bombs over the Soviet Union) would be in direct contravention of the 1967 Space Treaty and the 1974 ABM Treaty. And even to test the device in the atmosphere (which, if the weapon is to be developed, will surely happen) would strike at the heart of the very first nuclear test ban treaty signed a generation ago, in 1963, by the United States, Britain and the Soviet Union. For an American Administration flagrantly to flout one of the few arms agreement deals that has actually worked, would obviously be politically unacceptable. Today, the 'non-nuclear' character of SDI is being emphasized.

In its annual progress report on SDI to Congress in 1985, the Pentagon stated that "emphasis in the SDI program is being given to non-nuclear weapons for defense". The only mention made of a nuclear dimension to the programme is contained in a veiled reference to what the Pentagon calls, "nuclear-driven systems". Nevertheless, the Pentagon asked Congress for $120 million to be spent on research into X-ray lasers in 1985, $150 million in 1986, and $175 million in 1987, 1988 and 1989, which, with the $100 million already allocated in 1984, represents a total of nearly $900 million over a five-year period (1984–89) – twice the sum that will be spent on developing the more technologically advanced high-energy chemical lasers.

Most of this money will be directed to the Lawrence Livermore National Laboratory, nestled among the East Bay foothills, some 40 miles east of San Francisco. Here, government scientists were working on X-ray laser weapon research long before Star Wars, and today at the Lawrence Livermore Laboratory are to be found some of the most passionate advocates of SDI. Much of the work of the Laboratory is top secret, and reports that have filtered through to the press have differed on how far advanced this research is. Certainly, the problems in producing an X-ray laser (which British physicists Dr Leslie Allen and Dr Norman Dombey, writing in *New Scientist* September 1985, say no one has yet succeeded in producing) are immense.

There are three basic problems that a potential X-ray laser weapon system, if it is to work, must overcome. First, is the need to produce enough energy to create the X-rays. Second, is the problem of stationing the weapon in space, and third is the problem of targeting the weapon on to attacking missiles (or warheads).

The first problem is answered, in theory, by exploding a nuclear device powerful enough to produce a short but intensely bright burst of radiation at X-ray wavelengths. Experiments conducted at the US underground nuclear test centre under the Nevada desert, such as that carried out on March 23, 1985, have shown the second problem with X-ray lasers – how to focus the X-rays on to a target – have also been partially answered. Mirrors to concentrate the laser beam produced by such an explosion are not needed. Instead, a series of rods would direct the destructive beam on to a missile in a matter of a microsecond, penetrating the shiny metal skin of the booster and playing havoc with the missiles' guidance system. Focusing itself need not be as precise as with other forms of laser weapons. Indeed, an X-ray laser beam the width of two football fields would still, say some scientists, be powerful enough to penetrate and destroy its target. Others fundamentally disagree. To this group of scientists, X-ray lasers are so 'soft' that they would not penetrate the atmos-

Below: *Testing nuclear weapons in the atmosphere is banned by treaty, but before 1963 the US carried out tests over the Pacific to study the effects of EMP.*

phere (which might be necessary in order to strike at missiles during their boost phase), and the blow that they punch is one against which the missile could easily be protected.

Basing such a system would not in itself present nearly as many problems as those associated with other forms of lasers. The system could either be popped-up (as we have seen) – that is, launched from submarines placed close to Soviet missile silos (thus intercepting the missiles in their boost phase) – or they could be placed permanently in space to orbit over the target missile silos. To launch even a 3.5 megaton nuclear device presents few problems: certainly none that could not be overcome using existing systems (rockets

or even the shuttle). Of course, as even the most convinced of the star warriors admit, such a scheme might not be politically acceptable, so the pop-up system is likely to win in the end.

The X-ray laser is a system which seems – apart from political and ethical considerations, which exert little restraint upon many Star War advocates – to fulfil many of the objectives spelled out by President Reagan in his Star Wars speech on March 23, 1983. Certainly, it is a system which, despite official statements to the contrary, still holds the centre of the stage in Star Wars research and development programmes. Yet, despite its popularity, the system does suffer from a number of drawbacks,

no less important than the drawbacks facing other Star Wars weapons systems. Briefly, these are: the time constraints in launching the system to meet any actual or potential attack; the tendency of X-ray radiation to cripple all space systems, friend and foe alike over a considerable distance in space (and on Earth); their inability to penetrate the atmosphere, which means that they could not be used against a missile under an operational ceiling of some 65 miles (105km); and the central contradiction which lies at the heart of the whole enterprise: that of using nuclear weapons in order to make, in President Reagan's words, nuclear weapons 'impotent and obsolete'.

It seems unlikely, for the technical

reasons outlined, that X-ray laser weapons will form the crucial first line of defence against missiles in their boost phase. But this does not mean that faith in the X-ray laser as a space weapon has faltered. As the Pentagon budget allocations indicate, belief in the X-ray laser is even stronger today than it was when Dr Edward Teller first sold the idea to Ronald Reagan in 1982–83. Its role is now seen as being perhaps more viable as a weapon against missiles in their

Below: *At Los Alamos Laser Research Facility two converging carbon dioxide lasers, concentrating 25 trillion watts, are fired at a target the size of a full stop.*

post-boost phase or even in their mid-course phase rather than in their boost phase. Some reports even suggest that X-ray lasers are being considered as an anti-satellite or 'counter-defensive' weapon. Such a weapon could, it is argued, be used against a Soviet 'Star Wars' system – should such a system ever be deployed. For this role, the X-ray laser would be used to destroy Soviet defensive battle stations in space in order to let US retaliatory missiles through.

Whatever the outcome of this debate, it seems likely that scientists at the Lawrence Livermore Laboratory will continue their testing and experimentation in the hope that, one day, they will come up with a weapon that will replace the current generation of nuclear weapons. This 'third generation' weapon says Dr Roger Batzel, Director of the Lawrence Livermore Laboratory, is best described in the following way: 'The A-bomb is one million times as effective as high explosive. The H-bomb is 1,000–10,000 times as effective as the A-bomb. *Beam weapons could be one million times as effective as the H-bomb.*" It is a challenge which few at Lawrence Livermore see as anything but necessary. In the logic of mass murder a weapon is best judged not by the numbers it can kill or the suffering and destruction it will cause, but by the morally neutral notion of how *effective* it can be.

Above: *Laser power burns a hole through titanium – thicker than the outer skin of an ICBM, at Kirtland AFB, New Mexico.*

Particle Beam Weapons

Work on these weapons, which, in theory, follow the same principles as lasers, began in 1958 when the United States first thought of devising an anti-ballistic missile system. Progress has been slow, and today, nearly thirty years later, a prototype weapon has not yet been produced.

Particle beams are streams of atoms or subatomic particles which, when accelerated under laboratory conditions, are capable of reaching nearly the speed of light. To achieve such speeds would, some scientists claim, require massive machines 2 miles (3.2km) long and 4 miles (6.4km) wide. Their relevance to any space-based weapons system capable of being deployed in the near, or foreseeable future is therefore limited. Even a machine capable of accelerating particles to just half the speed of light would weigh 500 tons, and hundreds, if not thousands, of these 'machines' would have to be lifted into orbit if they were to provide a viable defence against nuclear missile attack.

There are two types of particle beam weapon currently being researched in the United States and the Soviet Union: charged particle beam

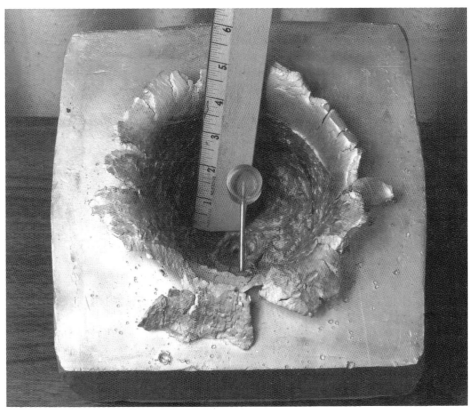

Above: *The damage that can be done to a cast aluminium block when a 7-gram pellet fired from a gas gun hits it at a speed of 23,000 feet per second.*

weapons and neutral particle beam weapons. Each has its advantages and disadvantages, although both also share a number of drawbacks that makes deployment of such weapons as part of SDI most unlikely. To destroy a missile in flight, a charged particle beam weapon would have to fire a stream of energetic particles, such as protons, through the atmosphere (if it hoped to destroy the missile in its boost phase) in order to disrupt the semi-conductors in the missile's guidance system — the only part of a missile vulnerable to particle beam attack. But such a task, say sceptics, is physically impossible. And the reason for this is simple. Such a weapon could never be properly aimed at its target because a charged particle beam would always be 'bent' by the Earth's magnetic field. To penetrate the atmosphere, a *neutral* particle beam would have to be fired. But such a beam (using hydrogen atoms, for example) would also suffer from problems of aim and could, in any case, only work against a target above an altitude of 93 miles (150km), because of the action of air molecules and again (though in a less strenuous way) because the Earth's magnetic field would cause the beam to spread out. Even if a neutral beam were to hit a missile rising through the

atmosphere, there is a very simple way in which the missile could avoid destruction. This is by protecting its guidance system with gallium arsenide semi-conductors which are 1,000 times more resistant to radiation damage than silicon semi-conductors.

Because of the ineffectiveness of such a weapon against a missile in its boost phase, there are numerous proposals to use the weapon against missiles (or warheads) in their post-boost or mid-course phase. But even here an electrically charged particle beam would be bent by the Earth's magnetic field to such an extent that accurate aiming would be virtually impossible. Neutral beams might be used, but there would be huge problems of accelerating, aiming and focusing the charged particles by electromagnets, then 'stripping' off the charge just before the beams were fired against the target. Creating the technology to accomplish such a feat might be decades away from now. Why, then, one might ask, are particle beam

weapons being developed?

There are several possible answers to this question, though none can be stated with any degree of confidence. First, if particle beams could be harnessed and a viable weapon made, then they *might* prove to be a better bet than other forms of beam weapon (such as chemical lasers) because they can more reliably 'kill' a missile. But as we have seen, there are relatively simple counter-measures that could be taken to protect a missile. Second, particle beam weapons could be made to operate in the atmosphere at short range. A research programme for the US Navy, code-named Chair Heritage, aims at producing a short-range weapon suitable for ship defence. And at the Lawrence Livermore Laboratory, scientists have been toiling since 1958 to devise an electron beam weapon for use in terminal-phase defence. The idea is to site an electron beam gun on the ground close to a missile silo or city to shoot beams at nuclear warheads as they re-enter the atmosphere. But this much smaller weapon would also encounter the same problems of aim and control of the beam. And the cost of developing just this small (terminal phase) part of a ballistic missile defence would carry a price tag of some $20 billion.

A more obvious reason why interest in particle beam weaponry continues might simply be because research has now gone on for so long that there are too many vested interests involved to want to stop it. Those engaged in the research naturally have good reason to see it continue. And in the climate of opinion that seems to exist in the United States today there is a willingness to fund almost any project that might provide a ballistic missile defence.

Kinetic Energy Weapons
There is nothing subtle about the way in which a kinetic energy weapon works. Like the cannon ball of old, it simply smashes into the target, destroying it by sheer force of impact. But the speed at which today's projectiles hit their target almost defy the imagination. In experiments conducted in the United States, an object weighing 0.1oz (3g) has been fired from an electromagnetic launcher at a velocity of 6 miles per second (10km/sec). Theoretically, say the scientists involved, it is possible to

shoot a 0.09oz (2.5g) object to a velocity of 31 miles (50km) per second using the same equipment – a 'distributed rail gun'. This piece of modern technology, 12yd (11m) long, is just one of the prototypes being produced by eight companies as part of the Star Wars scheme. As Dr Ian McNab, chief scientist with Westinghouse (one of the companies involved) says: "Electromagnetic guns don't need explosives and would be impossible to deflect. No matter where it hit a missile, it would destroy it." Because of this belief, and the fact that the electromagnetic rail gun could be workable years before the laser, it has been heralded by some as *the* 'wonder weapon' of the future: simple in concept and deadly in use.

Electromagnetic rain guns are not the only type of kinetic energy weapon being developed in the United States. Broadly, research centres on two types of weapon which differ only in the way in which they are propelled. The first, 'conventional' type, is launched by chemical rocket; the second propelled by electromagnetic force. Both offer a technology that could, conceivably, be used as part of a ballistic missile defence.

'Conventional' kinetic energy weapons

At 11.29 GMT on Sunday, June 10, 1984, two objects, each 3ft (0.9m) long and 18in (46cm) wide, smashed into each other at a speed of over 13,670mph (22,000km/h), 100 miles (161km) above the Pacific Ocean. One was a curious-looking metal umbrella, code-named the 'Homing Overlay Experiment (HOE) vehicle', fired from the US Mech Island missile range at Kwajalein Atoll, in the Marshall Islands. The other was a dummy nuclear warhead from a Minuteman ICBM launched 4,500 miles (7,242km) away from Vandenberg US Air Force base in California.

The collision was the climax of a research programme begun six years earlier by the US Army's Ballistic Missile Defense team, headed by Major General Elvin R. Heiberg II. With a budget of $300 million, Heiberg's task was to create a ballistic missile defence within the constraints laid down by the 1972 ABM Treaty. This involved assembling a system of hardware, software, guidance equipment and target-acquisition radar to locate, intercept and destroy

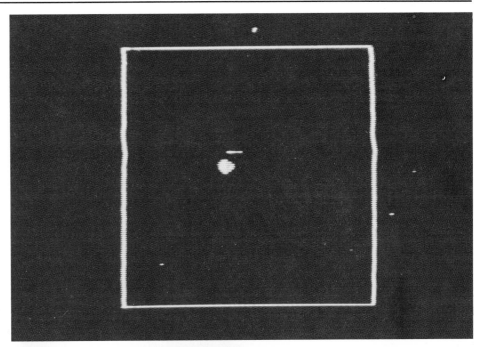

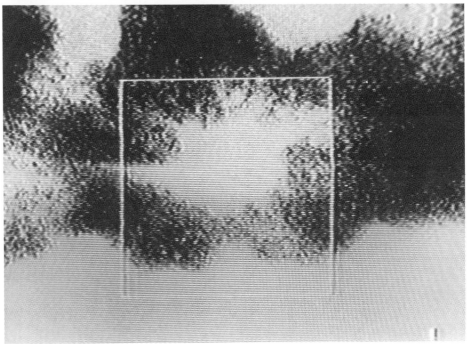

an ICBM's warhead.

The wonder of the system is the HOE vehicle itself. Within its squat, cylindrical shape are contained eight infra-red telescopes, a laser gyroscope, a mini-computer and 56 miniature booster rockets to position and lock the vehicle on to its target. Wrapped round the outside of the vehicle are 36 7ft (2m) long high-tension aluminium spokes, each studded with metal weights. As the vehicle homes in on its target, longwave infra-red sensors (capable of detecting human body heat 1,000 miles [1,609km] away) releases a switch to unlock the spokes which spring out to form a

Two frames from a video display of the interception of an ICBM warhead by the US Army's HOE vehicle, June 10, 1984.

metal 'net' or umbrella, 15ft (4.5m) across to 'catch' the approaching warhead. In the experiment of June 10, 1984, this device, though activated, was not needed. The two objects hit each other, precisely nose to nose.

The technical achievement was immense. It showed that it was possible to track down, intercept and destroy a nuclear warhead speeding through space at thousands of miles an hour, or as Amoretta Hoeber, Principal Deputy Assistant Secretary of the Army, described it, "we tried to hit a bullet with a bullet, and it worked". The confidence shown by the star warriors seemed, this time, to have been well founded. But as critics were quick to point out, the system had been tried three times before and failed, and knocking out one warhead after months of careful preparation and at a pre-arranged rendezvous was rather different from eliminating thousands of warheads and decoys careering through space in a real attack.

The three previous tests (the first on February 7, 1983, the second on May 28, 1983 and a third on December 16, 1983) had suffered, according to official government sources, from 'minor anomalies in a sensor cooling sub-system . . . random failure in the guidance electronics . . . softwear problem in the HOE's on-board computer'. These were dismissed as minor 'teething problems'. As the same source emphasized, 'the first three flights together satisfied more than 90 per cent of the data requirements for the program'.

The HOE is just one of the US Army's contributions to what is known, with the US military's mania for acronyms, as SDIP (Strategic Defense Initiative Program). 'Satka' is another of its research programmes: Surveillance, Acquisition, Tracking, Kill Assessment, which in layman's language means developing the means to detect, track and discriminate between objects in all phases of a ballistic missile's flight. KEW (kinetic energy weapons) forms another feature. With the success of HOE, the Army has set its sights on ERIS – Exoatmospheric Re-entry vehicle Interceptor System – which, should the decision to field a BMD (ballistic missile defence) be taken, will result in an operational weapon based on HOE's technology but launched by a much smaller missile.

ERIS aims at destroying RVs (re-entry vehicles) at the terminal stage, and the first step in the Army's programme is to acquire an early warning system. This programme, known as AAOA (Army Airborne Optical Adjunct) will provide airborne infra-red sensors to back up ground-based radars. In this larger programme, the HOE experience will prove invaluable. For

already the Army are confident that they have demonstrated the feasibility of infra-red identification and tracking, and of kinetic energy (KE) 'kill'.

In addition to HOE, the United States has also demonstrated the feasibility of KEW with the Vought MHV (Miniature Homing Vehicle) launched by the F-15 fighter. Though as we have seen, the system is essentially designed as an ASAT (anti-satellite weapon), it could also be

To defeat Soviet attempts to outfox SDI defences by launching ICBMs with fast-burn boosters that cut off at about a minute at low altitudes, the SDIO is conducting research into rail guns capable of firing projectiles at hyper-velocity. Beginning in the autumn of 1984 tests have achieved a firing rate of five projectiles within 0.5 seconds. Low-mass particles have achieved speeds of 40km/sec.

used, say the experts, as a weapon against RVs in the terminal phase of a ballistic missile defence, given refinements in the system's speed, guidance accuracy, and manoeuvrability. The Soviets too have their kinetic energy weapon in the shape of their ASAT system. But interest in both the USA and the USSR is focusing on firing KE projectiles, not by conventional chemical rocket, but by gigantic electromagnetic cannons or 'rail guns'.

Electromagnetic rail guns

At the University of Texas's Center for Electromechanics, scientists working on a prototype electromagnetic rail gun were reported, in the spring of 1985, to have fired a minute one-hundredth-of-a-gramme ball of metallic plasma to a velocity of 131,233 feet per second (89,477mph or 143,968km/h). Funded by the Armament Research Development Center of Dover, New Jersey, to the tune of $800,000, the ultimate aim of the two-year project is to achieve a velocity of 164,000 feet per second (111,818mph, 179,915km/h). By the

end of 1985 another weapon will be tested capable of firing ten 2.8oz (80 gramme) shells in one-sixth of a second at a speed of 6,500 feet per second (4,432mph, 7,131km/h).

In a special animated film produced by the High Frontier group to sell the idea of Star Wars to the American public, the electromagnetic rail gun has pride of place. The cartoon makes it look so simple. Patrolling space, these non-nuclear gun ships would fire small discs shaped like hockey pucks at a fantastic rate and at an incredible speed at attacking Soviet missiles, 'buses' and warheads. But the size of such gun ships, if one were ever to be built, would have to be hundreds of feet long in order to fire projectiles at the sort of speeds the cartoonists envisage. In fact, they would be more like aircraft carriers than gun ships. Fine under laboratory conditions, but not only impossible to place in space at present, such monstrosities would be a sitting duck to an enemy.

The weapon itself is huge. It consists of two giant parallel rails which form an electrical circuit. Powerful

Above: *Interception and destruction of nuclear-armed re-entry vehicles by a space-based electromagnetic rail gun is illustrated in this artists conception.*

bursts of electric current are used to create a magnetic field to drive projectiles called 'smart rocks' along the rail at immense speed. Each smart rock is a minor miracle of engineering. It consists of a metal 'shell' powered by tiny booster rockets and a miniature guidance system to home in on its target. Smashing into its victim at a speed of tens of thousands of miles per hour (created by the combined velocities of both objects), the target shatters into a shower of metal dust.

To produce even greater speeds, scientists have created (under laboratory conditions) the 'distributed rail gun'. Here, the projectile travels along the barrel of the gun and is accelerated by a series of mini-magnetic fields created at various stages along the barrel. As the projectile approaches, energy is switched on. When the projectile has passed through, the energy is switched off. As it passes through each stage, the velocity of the projectile is increased to speeds of 31 miles per second (50km/second). (This compares with a speed of 1,640yd per second [1.5km/second] achieved by the MHV launched by conventional chemical rocket by the F-15 fighter.) The longer the rail and the more accelerating stages, the faster the projectile travels.

The technology of electromagnetic machines has been the subject of interest to scientists for a long time. In the United States, for example, the USAF has been looking into the possibility of creating such a machine to replace steam catapults used on aircraft carriers to launch jet aircraft. Another proposed application is the launching of space probes. But it was the possibility of harnessing electromagnetic forces as a possible antiballistic missile (and satellite) weapon that attracted the multi-million dollar funding by the Department of Defense. In 1984 alone, $35 million was spent on electromagnetic rail gun 'research'.

Advocates of the rail gun claim that it is a device that can be used in the boost, post-boost and mid-course phases of a ballistic missile attack. To knock out most of the missiles in the boost phase would require a fleet of orbiting rail guns able to select, aim and fire smart rocks at the rate achieved by the Texas University prototype at a fraction of a second. And each projectile would have to home on to its target under its own guidance system – and the technology to do that is way into the future.

Defence in the mid-course phase would have to deal with thousands of fast-moving warheads and decoys. If the rail guns could not cope with this number, then some method of discriminating between warheads and decoys would have to be found: the projectiles would need to be more than 'smart' – they would have to be intellectual giants.

A daunting task and one which scientists such as Dr Henry Kolm of Electromagnetic Launch Research Incorporated, admits is 'severe'. Nevertheless, Dr Kolm is confident that many of the problems will be solved by the new technologies being developed such as 'homopolar

generators' and new light alloys. In the competition stakes to see which weapon wins the biggest slice of the SDI cake, the electromagnetic rail gun, once a rank outsider, is now attracting a growing body of backers. Says Dr Harry Fair of DARPA, "When President Reagan made his 'Star Wars' speech . . . we were only just realizing the potential of electromagnetic launchers. At that time [March 1983], laser or particle beam devices seemed the only credible systems for knocking out Soviet missiles in space. Since then, we have begun to realize that electromagnetic laun-

chers could be just as effective, if not more so."

Whatever the merits of the electromagnetic rail gun, or any other form of kinetic energy weapon, they are all severely handicapped by limited range and speed. To reach the speeds of lasers (185,000mph, 297,729km/hour) is beyond the realms of possibility. To take on the entire Soviet fleet of ICBMs, any defence, if it aimed at eliminating most of the attacking missiles, would have to succeed in the first few crucial moments of the attack. To do this, kinetic energy weapons are non-starters. But

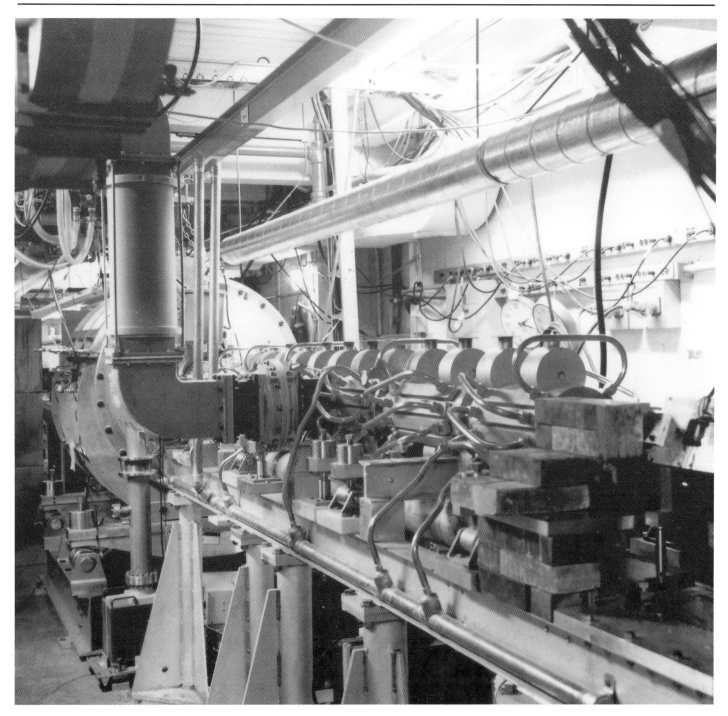

Above: *An experimental device to test the feasibility of using ground-based lasers to fire beams on to targeting mirrors in space.* Left: *An electromagnetic launcher code-named Checkmate.*

they could and probably will, if the system is deployed, be used as a back-up system to cover post-boost and mid-course interception, in addition to the range of laser weapons at the disposal of such a defence in the distant future.

In the ever expanding world of wonder weaponry, fresh instruments of death are revealed almost daily. Today, it's the gamma-ray laser – much more powerful than the X-ray laser and much more efficient. And for tomorrow, there's the curiously named device, dubbed the 'anti-matter bomb' – curious because bombs have always been destructive of matter. But this bomb is in some ways different. According to Dr Harry Nuckolls, head of the physics department of Lawrence Livermore Laboratory, it does not kill its victims, it just stuns and confuses them. This benign state is induced by exposing victims to massive doses of long wavelength radiation of great strength created by concentrating and directing the power from a nuclear explosion into the electromagnetic spectrum. Its effect on an enemy would be to render them impotent to wage war.

Whichever weapon system, or combination of weapon systems is chosen as a credible ballistic missile defence, for the system to work at all components will be required that are not weapons themselves. These other components make up what has come to be known as 'battle management'.

BATTLE MANAGEMENT

If the final war takes place in space, it will be fought by machines, not men. Man would be redundant in the short, sharp, terrifying action that, in just a few moments, would decide the fate of the Earth. Deciding what to do and how to respond to the first signs of a nuclear attack — which itself could only be sighted by early warning satellites — would allow no time for human deliberation. If a ballistic missile defence was to be even partially effective, it would have to locate, intercept and destroy thousands of missiles in the first few minutes, if not seconds (given improvements in Soviet ICBM technology), of the conflict.

The elaborate chain of command on which defence of the West now rests, beginning with early warning (EW) satellites alerting NORAD of a Soviet missile strike, and ending with the President of the United States who in theory will decide whether to push the button, would be totally redundant should a Star Wars defence ever be erected. When the chips were down, that decision could only be taken by

an anonymous, 'intelligent' machine. The sheer speed with which the defence would have to be activated could not cope with the creaking process of political decision-making. From this, two fundamental questions arise: is the creation of such a system technically *possible* and is it *desirable*? To perform all the functions necessary to wage war in space, an efficient battle management would have to:

1. Warn the defensive system of an attack
2. Calculate the number, trajectories and range of the attacking missiles
3. Locate and track the missiles
4. Assign, aim and fire the defensive weapons
5. Assess whether interception has been successful, or not
6. Re-assign the weapons to fresh targets and fire the defensive weapons against those missiles that got through
7. Alert the next stage(s) of the defence of the number, range and

trajectories of those missiles or warheads that had eluded the first line of the defence.

To deal with the scale of the attack the Russians could launch would require an automated system consisting of millions, if not billions, of lines of error-free coding: a feat which many scientists doubt is feasible. The system would have to be free of 'bugs' which notoriously plague all untried computer systems. The Star Wars system could never be properly tested: wartime use would be first-time use. "People are expecting too much of computers," says Dr Henry Thompson, head of Edinburgh University's advanced computer centre. "No one has any idea how to get there [to the stage of producing computers to control a Star Wars system]. And if someone claimed that he could devise such machines there would be no way he could devise a test that would convince you he was right."

Few doubt that, given sufficient time and money, the machines could be built. But the scale of the enterprise

Left: *To wage war in space super-sophisticated sensors will have to be able to detect, track and discriminate between warheads, decoys and debris.*

is collosal. The problems that would have to be overcome include:

1. The writing and designing of the error-free computer coded programs. In a report published by the Union of Concerned Scientists in the United States, the panel of nine scientists (including Professor Hans Bethe, Richard Garwin and Professor Carl Sagan) concluded that "experience with earlier defense system software, as well as examples from non-defense experience, suggests that it will be exceedingly difficult, if not impossible, to construct software that would operate properly in the environment of a nuclear attack, for which it could never have been fully tested."

2. The production of a system capable of handling the complex task of tracking and discriminating between real targets and decoys and assigning defensive weapons to them. This will include interpreting and responding to information relayed by sensors reporting on the range, velocity and manoeuvrability of the targets; the aiming, firing and damage evaluation of the defence and the reassignment of the weapons systems to other targets.

To take just one of the problems involved, that of discrimination between decoys and real targets: the coded program to do this will have to be prepared long before conflict breaks out, and be embedded in the software (and possibly in the hardware). If the attack was to change its system of decoys or deploy systems the defence was not prepared for (which seems likely), then the system would fail. It will always be open to the offense to devise ways of outfoxing the defence.

Nevertheless, vast sums of money are being pumped into researching a

Below: *Teal Ruby aims at providing the USAF with 'real time' surveillance of the Earth from space by using infra-red sensors.*

Above: A SAC B-52 bomber crew scramble during an exercise. How able is the system to cope with a real life alert?

computerized system able to deal with the sorts of problems outlined. One such project is Teledyne's Pentagon-funded 'Validator'. 'Validator' is a three-phased programme in which the initial project (costing $50 million) is to provide a longwave infra-red sensor for space surveillance, target acquisition, and pointing and tracking for a space-based laser weapon. Experiments will involve testing equipment onboard the space shuttle. As a Department of Defense official said, such a sensor "would apply directly to anti-satellite or defensive satellite systems", as well as ballistic missile defence. Later stages of the programme will include the testing of a 'hit-to-kill' device (a hydrogen or deuterium fluoride laser operating at 2 megawatts), which, it is rumoured, might also be fired from the shuttle.

As with other aspects of the Star Wars programme, hopes are pinned on new technology arising to solve the problems. *Teal Ruby*, a multi-billion dollar project begun by Rockwell International in 1977 aims at creating a revolutionary 'staring mosaic array' infra-red sensor, more sophisticated than the current 'scan-

ning' device used, for example, by the Defense Support Program's Early Warning Satellites. According to DARPA Director Dr Robert S. Cooper, *Teal Ruby,* unlike any previous sensor, would be able to distinguish between the Earth's 'natural clutter' and 'reflections', and 'real targets'. It would, said Cooper, "give the opportunity to [develop] low Earth-orbiting systems that can actually search for, detect and track", other satellites, objects in the atmosphere (including, it is claimed, cruise missiles), ships at sea and 'hot-objects' on the battlefield.

Teal Ruby is scheduled to be launched into orbit by the space shuttle *Discovery* in 1986, as part of the USAF's Space Test Program. The satellite, called AFP-888, will orbit the Earth at an altitude of 460 miles (736km) and be used to track an AF aircraft. In addition to tracking 'enemy' bombers, DARPA scientists hope to 'demonstrate the ability to detect and track much dimmer targets such as cruise missiles'.

The ability of a fully automated battle management system, however, to cope with the billions of instructions demanded of it must remain a matter

of serious doubt. Even with the present, comparatively simple, nuclear war alert system deployed by the United States, serious errors do, and have, occurred. On June 3, 1980, a computer at NORAD relayed a message to Strategic Air Command Headquarters (SAC) that two Soviet submarine-launched ballistic missiles had been fired at the United States: a message confirmed only seconds later with news that further missiles had been launched. Immediately, B-52 bomber crews were scrambled and awaited the final order for take-off. That order never came. SAC awaited confirmation from NORAD, which in turn awaited satellite and radar confirmation. No such confirmation was made. Investigation subsequently carried out by NORAD revealed that the computer had suffered a malfunction due to a dud chip, made in Taiwan and costing 46 cents (34p). In this case human hesitancy prevented a real response being made to a false alarm. One shudders to think what might have happened had the entire system been computerized.

To the extreme annoyance of the SDIO, critics find it all too easy to point to all the potential flaws in the system. What they fail to grasp, say the spacemen, is that given the will and the means *anything* is possible. Against this are the strongly held views of many eminent scientists in the United States and Europe that Star Wars will not, and *cannot* work. David Parnas, a top computer scientist at Victoria University, Canada, and a member of a ten-member panel of advisors looking into the possibility of creating a super computer, says: "My judgement is that research in Star Wars is going to fail, and I believe this so strongly that I'm willing to stake my professional reputation on it".

Perhaps, sometime in the future, some form of SDI will be deployed. No one, apart from the present holder of the office of the presidency of the United States, seems to believe that it can ever be a total (100%) defence against an all-out nuclear attack. But, say the critics of the scheme, even if every projection and every device that President Reagan claims on its behalf were realized, it will still always be easier and cheaper for an aggressor to defeat the system. It is a charge which, if true, makes even research and development into a ballistic missile defence, let alone deployment, a pointless task. How the Soviets will respond, and what countermeasures they might take, is a subject to which we now turn.

Below: *Technicians at Rockwell International assemble the Teal Ruby telescopic sensor. The system is scheduled for launch in 1986.*

CHAPTER 5

'OUT THERE WHERE THE PEOPLE AREN'T'

Fred Iklé, US Under Secretary of Defense

"A perfect or near perfect defense (against inter-continental ballistic missiles) is not on the cards – any more than a cure for death is."

Professor Aston B. Carter, Harvard University

THE CONSTRAINTS placed upon military activity between the two great superpowers over the past forty years has been, to some members of the military and political establishments in both East and West, irksome in the extreme. If there were no more nuclear weapons, the world might once again be made safe for fighting an old-style 'conventional' war. Since such a scenario is not going to happen, the thought seems to have crossed the minds of some military strategists that such a war could be taken out of its Earth-bound, human, context — where war is nasty and messy and millions of people are killed — and fought out in space, 'where the people aren't'. Deep in space, war could achieve the impersonality, the excitement, of a computerized game, where 'zapping' space invaders can be done cleanly and efficiently at the flick of a switch and no one is hurt.

Such a wish no doubt lies behind the desire to make space the battle ground of the future. The ground rules for such a conflict were laid years before President Reagan made his Star Wars speech of March 23, 1983. What SDI has done, however, is to bring the possibility of extraterrestrial conflict ever closer.

The question that is most commonly asked by sceptics and by those who strive to stop an all-out arms race from developing in space, is 'will Star Wars work?' And the answer they arrive at after consulting various experts and authorities is 'no'. But as Professor Hans Bethe, a Nobel laureate in physics and a leading critic of SDI, made plain after a visit to the Lawrence Livermore Laboratory, 'the physics is all right'. But Bethe went on to say that fashioning the physics into an operational defence is another matter, and one which he (among many others) believes to be impossible in the near future. But even if the hugely ambitious engineering feat required to build a fully operational ballistic missile defence in space was accomplished, such a defence would itself be extremely vulnerable to Soviet attack, and every item of the defence open to cheap and dirty countermeasures. The question is not, 'will Star Wars work?', but 'what could the Soviets do to stop it from working?' And what the Soviets would do has been made plain on a number of occasions.

"The purpose of Star Wars", said General Nikolai Chervov of the Soviet general staff to western journalists in July 1985, "is to disarm the Soviet Union. If Star Wars continues, we shall have no choice but to take countermeasures, including the build-up of offensive nuclear arms."

To many in the West — at least to many newspapers in the West — the General's comments seemed to confirm basic Soviet aggressiveness. If Star Wars is purely defensive (and the President of the United States has always said that it is), what have the

Left: *An advanced communications satellite.* Above: *A DOD artist's impression of a Soviet space shuttle launch from Tyuratum.*

Soviets to fear? The answer was clear: they are against it because it thwarts their own, hostile, plans for a first strike against the West.

A simplistic view, perhaps, and one which makes no attempt at being objective — that is, trying to see things from the Soviet point of view. Consider the response were a Soviet

leader to appear before television cameras and announce: "Let me share a vision of the future that offers hope ... It is that we embark on a programme to counter the awesome American missile threat with measures that are defensive ... What if free people could live in the knowledge that their security did not rest upon the threat of instant Soviet retaliation to deter a US attack; that we could intercept and destroy strategic ballistic missiles before they reached our soil or that of our allies? Comrades, tonight we are launching an effort which holds the promise of changing the course of human history. There will be risks, and results take time. But with your support, I believe we can do it."

There is no doubt what the response in the West would be. In the words of US Secretary of Defense Caspar Weinberger, if the Soviets were to deploy a Star Wars system of their own, it would be "one of the most frightening prospects" imaginable.

Publicly at least, Soviet Star Wars is being taken very seriously by both President Reagan and Caspar Weinberger. To newsmen assembled to hear the President's proposals for the November 1985 summit conference with Soviet leader Mikhail Gorbachev, the President revealed that "the Soviet Union is about ten years ahead of us in developing a defensive system". And in a speech to the World Affairs Council of Philadel-

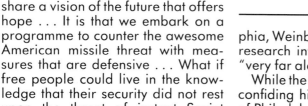

'Star Wars' was a key issue at the November 1985 summit conference.

phia, Weinberger claimed that Soviet research into strategic defence was "very far along".

While the Secretary of Defense was confiding his thoughts to the people of Philadelphia, Defense Intelligence Agency expert James McCrery was holding a press conference to launch a 27-page report published jointly by the Pentagon and States Department 'proving' the President's claims that the Soviet Union enjoyed a clear lead in Star Wars-type research and development.

Among the items contained in the indictment, is the claim that the Kremlin has spent ten times as much as the United States over the past ten years on 'strategic defence' – though the figure quoted includes Soviet spending on ASAT weapons, the Moscow ABM system, radar and civil and air defence expenditure in their calculations – items which are *not* included in the US costs. The Soviets are currently spending three times as much as the US on directed energy weapon research, says the report, and pinpoints those areas where the Soviets enjoy a lead:

1. A prototype 'fighting mirror' able to direct laser beams on to US missiles and warheads in space since 1978.

2. A kinetic energy 'gun' capable of shooting down missiles with metal projectiles operational since the 1960s.
3. A research programme in particle beam weaponry so advanced that much US work in this field has had to rely heavily on Soviet research culled from the pages of Soviet scientific journals.

There is little doubt among the experts that the Soviets have been heavily engaged in research into 'death-ray' weapons since the 1960s. However, few believe that this research is anywhere near translation into operational weaponry. United States Air Force Secretary Verne Orr, for example, casts doubt on whether the Soviets have an 'identifiable lead' in converting basic research into tangible systems. Even the Pentagon booklet itself admits that in the vital areas of target acquisition, tracking and firing, without which no space-based Star Wars system could work, "technologies ... are currently more highly developed in the West than in the Soviet Union". A lead which Defense Secretary Weinberger himself is anxious to keep by not allowing too many people into the secrets of Star Wars research.

If the Soviets should have a Star Wars defence ready for deployment before the American system, there is no doubt about what the American response would be. It would be the

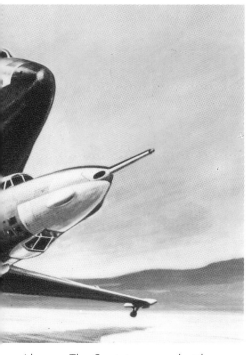

Above: *The Soviet space shuttle look-alike sitting astride a Bison bomber. Though first in space, the Soviets have been slow to develop their own shuttle system.*

same as the response of the Soviet Union today and of the United States government itself in the early 1970s when the Soviets installed their partial ABM (anti-ballistic missile) system around Moscow. Then, fearful that 'deterrence' would be destroyed, the United States set about increasing their strategic arsenal so that the intercontinental ballistic missile would get through – whatever defences were erected. It led, in part, to the development and deployment of MIRVs as a means of overcoming Soviet defences and to an increase in the number of America's nuclear warheads from 2,000 to over 7,000 in the next nine years.

The fear that the Soviets might decide to develop their own SDI is one which, though not a constant worry to members of the present Administration, is one they take sufficiently seriously to spend money (though the exact sum is not known, expenditure for 1986 is double that of the previous year) on what is known as the 'Advanced Strategic Missile Systems' programme. Operating from the 'Ballistic Missiles Office' at

Norton Air Force Base, California, the project is primarily concerned with developing a range of 'penetration aids' to confuse and frustrate a Soviet space-based ballistic missile defence, and to ensure that American missiles will always get through. According to a Pentagon spokesman, the office is also undertaking research into:

1. Developing small vehicles with radar signatures similar to those of RVs (Re-entry Vehicles) to confuse terminal-phase defence. In a test of the MX missile carried out over the Pacific, two of the ten RVs were part of the Advanced Strategic Missile Systems project.
2. 'Defence supression' systems designed to fool enemy radar by picking up signals and returning counter signals to fool the defence into 'thinking' that what are really decoys are warheads.
3. Development of an RV (Re-entry Vehicle) capable of manoeuvring in space to evade detection. These RVs will, it is planned, be installed in MX missiles and in the new mobile ICBMs currently being developed.
4. An advanced guidance system which will enable missiles to receive information from spy satellites and to change course in order to elude the defence.

The countermeasures to any space-based ballistic missile defence range from the crude to the sophisticated. But whatever the measure, they are all based on technology already in existence and are cheaper and easier to produce than any of the components of the defence. As Paul H. Nitze, chief arms-control advisor and negotiator to the Reagan Administration stated in February 1985, two criteria must be met before even a technically workable space-based BMD can be deployed. These are that the components of the defence must be capable of withstanding any attacks against it, and that Soviet

Left: *Soviet emphasis on long manned space flight is the prelude claim the Pentagon to orbiting space stations manned by military personnel.*

countermeasures must not be cheaper than the defence itself.

If the countermeasures were cheaper, this would mean that they could be built faster and on a larger scale than the proposed defence. There are three options open to the Russians to counter any Star Wars defence: they may try to *outfox* the system, *underfly* the system, or *overwhelm* the system; or they may opt to do all three at different stages of the defence.

OUTFOXING THE DEFENCE
The most crucial time for the defence is, as we have seen, the boost phase. If the defence can destroy most of the missiles before they have unpacked their warheads, then the later stages of the defence could cope with the

few warheads that managed to get through. To protect missiles at the boost phase an aggressor could do a number of things. He could shorten the boost phase by introducing fast-burning boosters. A reduction of the boost phase to a mere 40 seconds with an increase of only 15 per cent in the missile's weight is considered to be more than just theoretically possible. This would present an almost insurmountable difficulty for the defence. The missiles themselves could also be protected against penetration by lasers or at least greatly reduce the damage a laser could do by being smeared with a laser-deflecting coat. In addition, Richard Garwin has suggested that each booster could be equipped with a thin metallic sheet which, unfurled

Above: *Fired on a low trajectory from the Arctic Circle, the Soviet SS-NX-23 SLBM could underfly any of the Star Wars defences currently being proposed.*

at a high altitude, would absorb and deflect X-ray laser beams. Alternatively, a hydraulic cooling system or a moveable heat-absorbing ring could be employed which would protect the attacked area at the command of heat sensors.

More simply, the Soviets could launch an attack of fake missiles that behaved like boosters. The first wave of an attack could consist almost entirely of dummy ICBMs to exhaust the defence, since the defence would have to attack every object that

behaved like a booster. When this was over, the real attack could then be launched.

Since it is the missile that the defence has to eliminate and not the booster flame (which is all it has to aim at), aiming could be hampered by fluctuating the booster flame in an unpredictable way, by, for example, causing the missiles to spin like a rifle bullet, so that the laser would find it difficult to concentrate on one spot.

At each stage of the defence (boost, post-boost, mid-course and terminal), the attack could deploy vast numbers of decoys. As Richard D. Delauer, then Under Secretary of Defense for Research and Engineering, said to a committee of Congress in 1983, "any defensive system can be overcome with proliferation and decoys, decoys, decoys, decoys".

The range of decoys to deceive the defence is both extensive and ingenius. At the boost stage, decoys could take the shape of an ICBM but consist only of the booster rocket. One the missile reached near space and released its warheads, thousands of 'balloons', each made of plastic, shaped exactly like a warhead and covered by thin metal foil or wire mesh, could also be released. To the sensors used by the defence there would be no difference between decoys and the real thing. Each missile could carry as many, if not more, decoys than warheads. This would present tens of thousands of targets for the defence to contend with. Alternatively, the warheads themselves might be contained in

Above: *Called the Small Radar Homing Interceptor Vehicle this missile is intended to intercept RVs inside the atmosphere in the terminal phase of an SDI defence.*

balloons so that the swarm of objects travelling through space is again the same. So long as all the objects reflected (or emitted) the same radar signal to the defence, the defence would have no option but to move against all the objects – unless it had developed some kind of super-sensitive sensor able to distinguish between decoys and warheads. Metal fragments thrown up by the launch-vehicle itself, together with fragments from the fuel tanks, could also be used to provide 'radar reflectors' at virtually no cost at all.

In the mid-course phase, chaff — short strips of metal wire first used in World War II to confuse enemy radar — could be deployed in great clouds to blind and/or confuse the defence by putting up a vast area of radar reflection against which the RVs could not be 'seen'. Other decoys might be equipped with electronic devices to create radio 'noise', set at certain frequencies in order to jam the defensive radio system. Decoys containing nuclear material to confuse active sensors such as the proposed neutron probes, might also be deployed.

Decoys themselves, however, suffer from two principal faults. First, they are difficult to launch on to a 'convincing' trajectory (that is, the same trajectory as the warhead), and second, they slow down very rapidly when they approach the atmosphere, tending to burn up on re-entering. Nevertheless, decoys are effective enough to cause any proposed defence a lot of trouble.

UNDERFLYING THE DEFENCE
None of the proposals currently under consideration by the SDI Organization deals with a defence against submarine-launched ballistic missiles fired on a low trajectory, or against cruise missiles fired from the air (from bombers) or from submarines.

Fired from Soviet submarines off the United States coastline from launch points difficult to detect, a ballistic missile would take only three to five minutes to reach a target near the coast. By firing ballistic missiles at low trajectories from submarines, the boosters and warheads spend far less time in space (again making it difficult for lasers to operate) and greatly reducing the time the defence has to destroy the attack. None of the proposed space defence systems would be effective against such an attack, since almost all lasers are ineffective in the atmosphere.

Low-flying cruise missiles could also evade such a defence, although their slow speed might tell against them, unless that defence was

---

Below: Underflying SDI defences, the submarine-launched SS-NX-21 cruise missile can be fired from a standard size Soviet torpedo tube and has a range of 1,864 miles (3000km).

supplemented by a big improvement in the 'conventional' air defences of the United States. To strengthen air defences sufficiently to meet the increased number of Soviet cruise missiles and bombers, would cost, according to former Defense Secretary James Schlesinger, another $50 billion a year in addition to whatever was spent on Star Wars. Such a defence system is perfectly feasible — easier indeed than any proposed defence against ICBMs — but would be an essential though costly addition to any Star Wars defence against Soviet nuclear missile attack.

OVERWHELMING THE DEFENCE
Apart from the cost of building more ICBMs to overwhelm the defence, the number of warheads carried by the existing Soviet ICBM fleet could be greatly increased by what the experts call 'fractionation'. In a report to Congress, the US Joint Chiefs of Staff claimed that the formidable Soviet SS-18 ICBMs could easily increase their current 10 warhead payload, the maximum permitted by treaty, to a staggering 30 warheads per missile. If the Soviets were to launch just 1,000

missiles this would result in 30,000 warheads, apart from decoys, penetration aids, etc, whizzing through space, unless the defence had eliminated the bulk at the boost stage.

Simplest of all, perhaps, would be for the Soviets to mount a direct attack upon the extremely vulnerable components of the space-weapons system itself. This need not be costly (indeed it would be cheap) and presents few technical problems. To destroy the delicate mirrors that might be based in space would present no problem at all. And all that is needed to destroy an expensive orbiting laser battle cruiser is to launch a satellite in exactly the same orbit, but in the opposite direction. The 'warhead' could be any metal object – Arthur C. Clarke suggests a bucket of nails. Should the 'warhead' fail to intercept the target, it does not matter. An hour later the expanding

cloud of nails will again encounter the target, and if it does not destroy the target this time, again it does not matter for at every hour, on the hour, the nails will be offered another opportunity. Sooner or later, the orbiting laser battle station and the bucket of nails will meet. The celestial mechanics of motion makes such an encounter inevitable. It has been calculated that if a swarm of 1oz (28g) pellets was released into orbit by an orbiting satellite, each pellet would be capable of penetrating 6in (15cm) of steel – and much more if it were suitably shaped – at a speed of 24,856mph (40,000km/hour).

More drastically, the Soviets might decide to detonate a series of nuclear devices in space to blind the infra-red sensors used to detect their boosters. This would have the added advantage, from their point of view, of blacking out all radar. Alternatively, they might bide their time and set off a series of nuclear bursts ahead of a flight of RVs at an altitude of some 37 to 50 miles (60 to 80km) above the atmosphere. This would ionize an area of tens of kilometres in space, blinding the defence and 'hiding' the RVs for several minutes – sufficient time

for them to descend on to their targets. Space mines of the type being developed as ASAT weapons would make an equally effective weapon against the component parts of a Star Wars defence. The 'mine' might be disguised as a harmless communications satellite and parked close to its target, activated by remote control at any time before, during or after an attack.

Ground facilities used for battle management would be vulnerable to attack from ground-hugging cruise missiles, able to evade radar detection, as would communications and control centres and the basing facilities associated with a land-based 'pop-up' system of defence.

The Soviets make no bones about what they would do if a US BMD was to be deployed. In May 1984 a panel of six Soviet scientists listed the steps they considered the Soviet Union would take to render Star Wars 'useless'. Listed are those devices which they considered 'cheap and easy':

1. Clouds of heavy balls to hurl in the path of the defences.

Below: At the directed-energy research centre at Sary Shagan, Soviet military scientists are developing a ground-based laser that could be used for ballistic missile defence.

2. Camouflaging Soviet missile launchers.
3. Prevent US lasers from locking on to Soviet missiles as they rose from the ground.
4. Shooting down US Star Wars assets in space by small surface-based missiles similar to the US Sprint.
5. Deploy satellites armed with short-range missiles close to US space stations to be fired when necessary.
6. The use of ground-based lasers against US space stations.
7. Exhaust the supply of fuel to US laser battle stations by 'false missile launchings'.
8. The coating of Soviet ICBMs with special substances and the use of 'retro-reflectors' to confuse US lasers.

While not all of these counter-measures are either 'cheap' or 'easy', or even currently feasible (firing ground-based lasers against orbiting battle stations), they show the comparative complacency the Soviets feel in undermining any space-based BMD the United States might choose to erect. At the heart of Soviet suspi-cion is the fear that SDI forms part of an American determination to achieve a 'first strike' capability. Since the Soviets know from their own research into lasers and particle beam weapons that a total space-based defence against nuclear mis-siles cannot be constructed in the for-seeable future, they conclude that such a defence must be aimed at pro-tecting missile silos, centres of battle control and command, and com-munications. From the Soviet point of view, if such a thing were to happen (and also from an American point of view if the Soviets were themselves to deploy a Star Wars system), the scene would be set for a nightmare scenario.

In the event of conflict arising bet-ween the two superpowers, Super-power A attacks the missile silos and other top priority targets of Super-power B with the full force of its ICBM fleet. Superpower B, according to 'deterrence' theory, has only one of two options open to it. It can either

---

Below: *Boeing's design for a low-orbit Space Operations Center – a military C³I base.*

accept its own destruction, or it can retaliate and inflict mutual destruc-tion on the enemy. Since the whole structure of strategic thinking rests upon the belief that the only thing that prevents one superpower attacking another is fear of retaliation, it follows, logically, that Superpower B must unleash its full ICBM fleet against Superpower A. But if Super-power A has a ballistic missile de-fence, it might be able to destroy sufficient numbers of attacking mis-siles to be able to 'survive' Super-power B's attack. Indeed, if this were so, Superpower A might be tempted to launch an attack on Superpower B to achieve just this result.

Such is the belief at least of R. Z. Sagdeyev, who heads the USSR Academy of Sciences Institute of Space Research (Russia's NASA). "The very attempt", says Sagdeyev, "to create a space-based ABM de-fence system will become a heavily destabilizing factor in increasing the stimulus for the first pre-emptive strike and the growing danger of nuc-lear war." A view which is shared by President Reagan and Weinberger. In an interview published in *Time* in October 1985, Weinberger stated

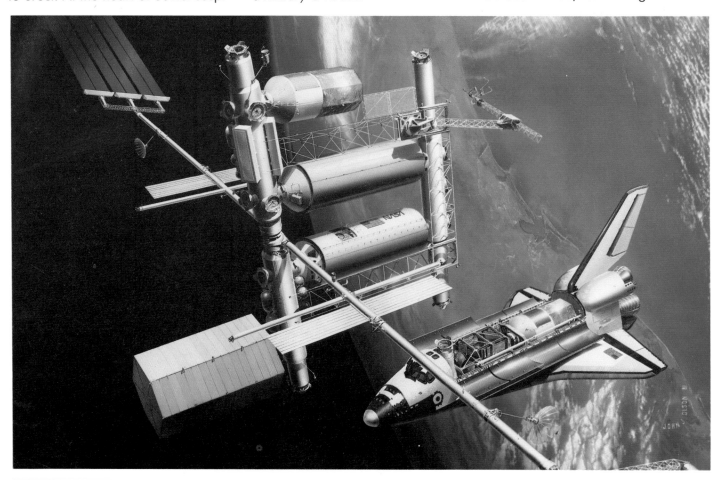

that "the President is aware that it [SDI] could be destabilizing if you give one side a shield that the other could not penetrate, and therefore that side would be safe to launch a war behind it. He [the President] said that if we find we can do this, before we deploy we would share it with the world." However, American mistrust of the Soviets is such that while Weinberger considers US possession of SDI is all right, Soviet possession is terrifying: "What kind of world would it be if the Soviets get this [SDI] without the slightest intention of sharing it with anybody?"

The view from Moscow is equally suspicious. American Star Wars, according to the Moscow line, is the final act of a drama which began with

the dawning of the space age. The American desire to dictate the terms is not new. "Only if the United States occupies a position of pre-eminence", declared President John F. Kennedy in 1961, "can we help decide whether this new ocean [space] will be a sea of peace, or a terrifying theatre of war."

Few analysts believe that the USSR will build its own Star Wars defence. It is not Moscow's style to act hastily or dramatically. There will be few visible signs of response at all – apart from table-thumping rhetoric. As with other weapons systems developed in the West, the Soviets will 'wait and see' – though they might, if they feel provoked, respond by fielding a space-based weapon long before it

Above: *With complex communities, such as this Boeing concept, engaged in vital scientific and industrial work in space, the need will arise for space forces to be deployed in the future to defend them.*

was properly operational and before the United States. Such is the view taken by Stephen M. Meyer of the Massachusetts Institute of Technology, and a consultant on Soviet military policy to the DOD. If SDI does go ahead, says Meyer, it will provoke the Soviet Union to become the "first in space with a laser. It won't be an effective weapon, but it will be a laser and it will drive Congress and officials . . . crazy."

"Like approaching storm clouds," wrote United Nations Secretary General Javier Perez de Cuellar in 1982, "[it] threatens to cut off all rays of hope: this is the increasing and rapidly escalating militarization of outer-space ... An arms race in space would increase the areas and the potential for confrontation, adding a new dimension to the human destruction that would stem from it."

With the development of a ballistic missile defence system by the United States, the prospect of space becoming the battle ground of the future has increased, in the view of many, at an alarming rate. The high ideals on which NASA was based have been corroded by the military space programmes it now undertakes. "I fear that as military space projects gobble up more funds," says Kosta Tsipis, of the Massachussetts Institute of Technology, "NASA will atrophy completely, and civilian work in space will atrophy with it."

The National Space Strategy signed by President Reagan in the summer of 1984 sets out 'major long-range national space goals'. While economic and scientific topics are covered, pride of place in the blueprint, which will carry the United States into the twenty-first century, is given to military matters. According to *Air Force* magazine, the plan will ensure "that the United States will enjoy routine, un-challenged and un-impeded access to space for whatever purposes it deems necessary, consistent with arms-control agreements, for the deterrence of and, if need be, the waging of war in space."

Such a strategy calls for:

1. Manned military operations in space.
2. New communications, surveillance, early warning, navigation and mapping satellites.
3. A new NASA/DOD launch vehicle to replace the Shuttle and capable of lifting 300,000lb (136,080kg) payloads into orbit.
4. The hardening of all space assets to withstand attack.
5. The deployment of a defensive force able to operate up to and beyond geosynchronous orbit.
6. The use of NASA's Space Station, scheduled for a 1991 launch, for military purposes.
7. The cultivation of techniques to enable crews to assemble platforms in space.
8. The deployment of 'orbital manoeuvring vehicles' and 'orbital transfer vehicles' for retrieving satellites in Earth-orbit and the transferring of satellites to the Shuttle and its successor for repair.

As the report states, few of these proposals are new, indeed many date back to the 1950s. Nevertheless, it recognizes that such steps are now realizable and that such an effort "springs in large measure from the Administration's Strategic Defense Initiative program".

The defence of increasingly complex military assets in space will in itself stimulate the militarization of space. When economic exploitation really gets under way, space enterprises, in the shape of commercial and scientific operations, will need military protection. The link that was forged in the eighteenth and nineteenth centuries on Earth between commerce and a military presence will be seen in space. Areas in space – as areas on Earth – will be defined as 'strategically vital' and defended. Piracy, which blossomed on the high seas, will become common in space. Space ships, similar to naval ships at sea, will have the job of 'policing' commercial vessels. And war, unless first eradicated on Earth, will inevitably occur in space.

Spacemen with an eye to the future are already formulating a strategy that will dictate the terms in which that war will be fought. Already in the United States, space forces have been established and there is growing clamour for a united Space Command to perform the same functions as carried out by other branches of the service: training, operation planning, equipment procurement, the devising of strategies, and the carrying out of exercises. Such activities are already being performed in the Soviet Union by the 'Anti-Space Defence Forces', a branch of the National Air Defence Force, by the Strategic Rocket Forces and by the Strategic Air Force which is responsible

Below: *By the year 2001 Lockheed envisage a space colony with zero-gravity modules for scientific, commercial and military use.*

Jack Olson

its power." It could count as a portrait of our age. Every day eight new nuclear warheads trundle off the production line of the nuclear bomb factories in the United States; a similar number are manufactured in the Soviet Union. Acquiring the means to exterminate life on Earth is big business. Over 200,000 people earn their daily bread in the United States alone by developing, producing, storing and plotting the use of nuclear weapons.

Treaties and agreements to limit their numbers are concluded only after difficult and painfully protracted negotiation which, in the eyes of many, achieve little. The human process which this demands — patience, compromise, trust and understanding — seem a shaky basis for security. Understandably, the wish that peace can be achieved without making any sacrifices, without having to compromise and accept another's point of view, is appealing. "The American pysche", writes James Schlesinger, "believes a perfect defense [against nuclear weapons] should be attainable". Such a belief, however, is illusory. "There is no hope for this in our lifetime," he concludes, "or in the lifetime of our children." It is a difficult truth to accept, for it means that the only defence is learning to control their use.

Over forty years ago, soon after the ending of the Second World War, in which over 50 million people died, Arthur C. Clarke spelled out the realities of the age in a prophetic essay entitled *The Rocket and the Future of Warfare.*

for cosmonaut training.

To wage war in space, new forms will have to be found for ancient military arts. Targeting, navigation, communications, command, control and intelligence activities will have to be performed by automatons and robots. Problems of weightlessness and physiological and psychological disturbance suffered by man in space will mean that most, if not all, vital functions will be carried out by machines. Human thought processes will be deemed too slow for the complexities of battle management.

None of the men now engaged in creating today's space forces underestimates the difficulties involved. But they share a touching belief in the old saying, 'necessity is the mother of invention': the means will be created so long as there is a need for them.

One such invention is the proposed 'Space Cruiser', a single-seat space-

Above: *Launched from the space shuttle the Orbital Transfer Vehicle will extend the USAF's presence deeper into space.*

plane designed to be launched from the Shuttle or larger 'space aircraft carrier', or on top of a Titan II or MX booster or their successors. Though dismissed by one Air Force general as "a one-man sneaky Pete in a Battlestar Gallactica", DARPA see the need for such a machine and have funded a feasibility study to look into research and development.

"Violence arms itself with the inventions of art and science in order to contend against violence," wrote von Clausewitz in 1832; "self-imposed restrictions, almost imperceptible and hardly worth mentioning, termed usages of international law, accompany it without essentially impairing

"The only defence against the weapons of the future is to prevent them ever being used. In other words, the problem is political and not military at all. A country's armed forces can no longer defend it; the most they can promise is the destruction of the attacker . . .

Upon us, the heirs, of all the past and the trustees of a future which our folly can slay before its birth, lies the responsibility no other age has ever known. If we fail in our generation, those who come after us may be too few to rebuild the world, when the dust of the cities has descended and the radiation of the rocks has died away."

GLOSSARY

AAOA [US] Army Airborne Optical Adjunct. High flying aircraft able to detect missiles at very long range using **IR** or optical sensors.

ABM Anti-ballistic missile. The 1972 ABM Treaty limits each superpower to one ABM site with 100 missiles. The Soviets have an operational ABM system around Moscow called *Galosh*. US developed two sites in 1960s but neither operational.

ALL Airborne Laser Laboratory – a converted Boeing 707 carrying an experimental high-energy chemical laser weapon mounted in a turret on upper fuselage. Designed as a potential **ASAT** weapon. Tests began in 1970s.

Apogee High point of a satellite's orbit when it is farthest away from Earth.

ASAT Anti-Satellite weapon. Russians possess an operational ASAT weapon of limited use and have placed a self-imposed moratorium on ASAT tests since 1984. The USA is currently testing the F-15/Vought ASAT system and is pressing ahead with deployment. Technologically related to **SDI.**

Battle Management The computerized 'high command' of **SDI** theoretically responsible for interpreting, analyzing and responding to any potential attack. Such a system (still in its infancy) will have to provide error-free information despite the fact that it can never be properly tested.

BMD Ballistic Missile Defence. Strictly a system designed to defend **ICBM** sites against missile attack. Commonly widened in meaning to include any anti-ballistic defensive system.

BMEWS Ballistic Missile Early Warning System radar stations (Thule, Greenland, Flyingdales Moor, England and Clear, Alaska). Developed by US in late 1950s to alert West of Soviet nuclear missile attack. In process of being updated with phased-array radar.

Boost phase First stage of a missile's flight, taking missile through Earth's atmosphere. Boost phase of contemporary **ICBM** lasts 3–5 minutes. Theoretically possible to reduce this to under 60 seconds.

Bus Term used for the post-boost vehicle of a ballistic missile carrying one or more warhead capable of independent manoeuvring.

C³I US military jargon for Command, Control, Communications and Intelligence.

Chaff Aluminium foil used to reflect radar signals. Large clouds of chaff will register similar radar

'signature' as target so act as effective decoy.

CSOC Consolidated Space Operations Center. USAF facility near Peterson AFB, near Colorado Springs. Due to open in December 1987, the Center will provide a single location for command and control of military satellite missions.

Cruise Low-altitude, continuously powered, winged missile that flies through the atmosphere.

DARPA [US] Defense Advance Research Project Agency. Headed by Robert Cooper, DARPA is responsible for funding many of the 'high-tech' **SDI** weapons research programmes.

DTST [US] Defensive Technologies Study Team. Under ex-NASA director James Fletcher, DTST presented President Reagan with a feasibility study on **SDI** in the autumn of 1983.

Electromagnetic railgun A **Star Wars** space-based **KEW** firing 60 'bullets' a second. No operational weapon exists though laboratory prototypes have been tested.

ELINT Electronic Intelligence.

Elliptical orbit An orbit in which the high and low points differ widely.

EMP Electromagnetic Pulse. The powerful current of intense electromagnetic energy released by a nuclear explosion.

EW Electronic Warfare or Early Warning [satellite].

ERIS Exoatmospheric Re-entry vehicle Interceptor System. Small US Army experimental ballistic missile for use in **terminal phase** defence.

FOBS Fractional Orbit Bombardment System.

FSSS Future Security Strategy Study. A second study group under Fred C. Hoffman set up by President Reagan to examine space-based **BMD.**

GEODSS Ground-based Electro-Optical Deep-space Surveillance System.

Geosynchronous orbit Also known as geostationary or Clarke orbit after Arthur C. Clarke who first suggested such an orbit in 1945. 22,300 miles [35,880 km] from Earth a satellite takes 24 hours to complete one revolution.

Ground track The projected path traced out by a satellite over the Earth's surface.

High Frontier   Right-wing American pressure group, founded by ex-US Army Lt. Gen. Daniel O. Graham. Early advocates of a space-based **BMD.**

HOE   [US Army] Homing Overlay Experiment. A **KEW** which destroys an **ICBM RV** in space by direct impact. First successful test June 10, 1984.

ICBM   Inter-Continental Ballistic Missile. Range 3000-8000 miles (4827-12,874 km).

IR (Infra-red)   Electromagnetic radiation beyond the red end of the visible spectrum.

IRBM   Intermediate-Range Ballistic Missile. Range 1800-3000 miles (2896-4827 km).

Kiloton   Equivalent explosive power of 1000 tons of TNT (trinitrotoluene).

KE   Kinetic Energy.

KEW(s)   Kinetic Energy Weapon(s). Small projectiles destroying target at phenomenal speeds by impact.

Laser   Acronym for Light Amplification by Stimulated Emission of Radiation.

LODE   Large Optics Demonstration Experiment. A 4m space-based mirror that aims and focuses a laser beam on to a moving target.

MAD   Mutual Assured Destruction. The doctrine that nuclear war is suicidal because neither superpower could attack the other without inviting certain retaliation and destruction.

MAS   Mutual Assured Survival.

MHIV   Miniature Homing Intercept Vehicle. USAF **ASAT** weapon launched by F-15 interceptor.

Mid-course phase   Third stage of an **ICBM's** flight lasting some 20 minutes.

MIRACL   Mid-Infra-Red Advanced Chemical Laser. A chemical laser developed in the late 1970s and first successfully tested under controlled conditions in 1985.

MIRV   Multiple Independently-targeted Re-entry Vehicle. See **Bus.**

MRV   Multiple Re-entry Vehicle.

MX   Three-stage solid fuel US **ICBM.** The 10-warhead missile specifically designed for attacks against Soviet command centres and underground missile silos. Three times as powerful and twice as accurate as Minuteman. Also known as the 'Peacemaker'.

NATO   North Atlantic Treaty Organization. Greeted President Reagan's **SDI** proposals with scepticism in 1983 but by December 1985 Britain, and in March 1986

West Germany, had signed up **SDI** commercial contracts and had politically endorsed **Star Wars.**

NASA   National Aeronautics and Space Administration.

Nautical mile   1.15 statute miles/1.852 km.

NORAD   North American Aerospace Defense Command. Established in the early 1960s under Cheyenne Mountain, near Colorado Springs and manned by USAF and Royal Canadian Air Force personnel. Mission is to determine whether SU has launched nuclear bomber/missile attack against North America. Also houses the space Defense Operations Center.

OMT   US military jargon for 'Other Military Target'.

Particle beam weapons   Streams of atoms or sub-atomic particles fired from space-based battleships at **ICBMs** in **post-boost** and **mid-course** phase at almost the speed of light.

Penetration aids   Devices released by **MIRVs** in **mid-course** phase to confuse defences. Could consist of dummy warheads, balloons, **chaff** or even pieces of missile debris.

Perigee   Low point of a satellite's orbit when it is closest to Earth.

Polar orbit   The path followed by a satellite passing over both poles of Earth.

Post-boost phase   Second stage of an **ICBM's** flight lasting up to six minutes. **MIRVs** are released from the missile and follow an independent ballistic trajectory to the target.

'Real time'   Live transmission to Earth from orbiting reconnaissance satellites.

R & D   US military jargon for Research and Development.

RV   Re-entry Vehicle. Cone-shaped vehicle containing nuclear warheads launched from **ICBM** which re-enter the atmosphere on to target after space flight.

SAC   Strategic Air Command.

SAINT   Satellite Interceptor, USAF **ASAT** project of early 1960s.

SALT   Strategic Arms Limitation Talks.

SAM   [Soviet] Surface-to-Air Missile.

Satellite Control Center   USAF facility at Sunnyvale AFB, California. Commands and controls military spacecraft through worldwide network of satellite tracking stations.

SATKA   Surveillance, Acquisition, Tracking, Kill Assessment. US Army Star Wars related **R & D** programme.

SDI   Strategic Defense Initiative.

SDIO   Strategic Defense Initiative Organization. Set up on April 1, 1984 under Lt. Gen. James A. Abrahamson charged with the task of implementing the **SDI.**

SDIP   Strategic Defense Initiative Program.

SLBM   Submarine-Launched Ballistic Missile.

SLCS   Space Launch Complex Six ['Slick 6']. The new USAF Space Command launch centre at Vandenberg Air Force Base, California. Future space shuttle launch site.

Smart rocks   Projectile, fired by **KEW** at speeds of up to 40 km/sec.

SPADATS   Space Detection and Tracking System. Worldwide US radar and optical surveillance system. Information from SPADATS fed into **NORAD** monitoring all artificial satellites and debris in Earth-orbit.

SSBN   Nuclear-powered ballistic missile submarine.

SS-N   [Soviet] Sea-launched surface-to-surface missile.

Star Wars   Popular name for **SDI** derived from George Lucas's futuristic science-fiction fantasy film of the same name.

Teal Ruby   Experimental **USAF Space Division** research programme funded by **DARPA** to demonstrate detection of aircraft in flight and differentiate Earth background information from the aircraft information.

Telemetry   Radio signals emitted from a rocket or satellite to a ground station.

Terminal phase   Fourth and final stage of an **ICBM**'s flight when **RVs** re-enter the Earth's atmosphere on to target.

USAF Space Command   Created September 1982. Space fighting force operating **ASAT** and **SDI** systems.

USAF Space Division   Part of USAF Systems Command and responsible for 'research, development, launch and on-orbit command and control of military space systems'. Space Division HQ, Los Angeles AFB, California. Commander Space Division also vice-commander USAF Space Command.

Left: *The Boeing Orbital Maneuvring Vehicle (OMV) will meet NASA's need for a reusable space tug in the 1990s. Launched from the space shuttle, the OMV could deliver and retrieve satellites up to a range of 2,000 miles (3,218km).*

FURTHER READING

Books

Air Force Magazine (ed). *Space Weapons* (Thames and Hudson, 1959)

Baker, David. *The Shape of Wars to Come* (Patrick Stephens, 1981)

Campbell, Duncan. *The Unsinkable Aircraft Carrier* (Michael Joseph, 1984)

Carter, Ashton B. *Directed Energy Missile Defense in Space* (MIT Office of Technology Assessment, April 1984)

Clarke, Arthur C. *1984: Spring* (Panther Books, 1985)

Delf, George. *Humanizing Hell* (Hamish Hamilton, 1985)

Dyson, Freeman. *Weapons and Hope* (Harper and Row, 1984)

Ford, Daniel. *The Button* (Allen & Unwin, 1985)

Graham, Lt. Gen. Daniel O. *We Must Defend America* (Heritage Foundation, 1983)

Jasani, B. *SIPRI Year Book 1985* (Taylor & Francis, 1985)

Karar, Thomas. *The New High Ground* (New English Library, 1984)

Langford, David. *War in 2080* (Westbridge Books, 1979)

Marsh, Peter. *The Space Business* (Penguin, 1985)

Peebles, Curtis. *Battle For Space* (Blandford, 1983)

Scheer, Robert. *With Enough Shovels* (Secker & Warburg, 1983)

Stares, Paul. *The Militarization of Space – US Policy, 1945–84* (Croom-Helm, 1985)

Thompson, E. P. (ed). *Star Wars* (Penguin, 1985)

Turnill, R. *Jane's Space Flight Directory, 1985* (Jane's, 1985)

Articles

Bethe, Hans A., Garwin, Richard L., Gottfried, Kurt, and Kendal, Henry W., 'Space-based Ballistic Missile Defences', *Scientific American,* Oct 1984

Broad, William J. Star Warriors *(Science Digest,* September 1985)

Garwin, Richard L., *et al,* 'Anti-satellite Weapons', *Scientific American,* June, 1984

Garwin, Richard L., and Bethe, Hans A., 'Anti-ballistic Missile Systems' *Scientific American,* March 1968

Union of Concerned Scientists. *The Fallacy of Star Wars* (New York, 1984)

Yonas, Gerold, Bethe, Hans A., and Zachariasen, Fredrik. 'Can Star Wars Make Us Safe?', *Science Digest,* September 1985

INDEX

A
AAOA, 78
Abalakova, 16
Abrahamson, James A., 50, 51-3, 58, 63
Abel, Brig. Gen. Richard F., 21
ABM Treaty, 1972, 46
ABM-X-3 system, 47
Aerospace Defense Squadron, 10th, 26
Advanced Strategic Missile Systems, 89
Aerojet General, 54
airborne optical system (AOS), 54
    defense system, 36
    test site, 16
Aldridge, Edward, 20, 27
Alice Springs, 11, 13
Allen, Leslie, 73
Allen Jr., General Lew, 28
Alpha, 70
Andropov, Yuri, 7
anti-ballistic missile (ABM), 26-27, 29, 39, 44-7
    test sites, 16
    defense system, 36
anti-matter bomb, 81
anti-satellite systems (ASAT), 19, 20, 23-37, 39, 79
Apollo Moon Programme, 12
Armament Research Development Center, 79
Atlas D-Agena B rocket, 24
Aviation Week & Space Technology, 15, 27, 30, 34, 35, 53

B
B-1 Bomber, 43, 46
Ballistic Missile Agency, 12
Ballistic Missile Defense (BDM) 29, 48-55, 78, 96
ballistic missile early warning system, 26
Ballistic Missiles Office, 89
Battle Management, 81-5
Batzel, Roger, 75
Baudry, Patrick, 63
'Beltway Bandit', 53
Bendetson, Karl, R., 8
Berliner, Hans, 64
Bethe, Hans, 27, 64, 83, 87
Biddle, Wayne, 57
Big Bird, 14, 15
'Big Blue Cube', 9
'Black Vault', 13, 14
BMEWS, 26
Boeing Aerospace Company, 21, 54
Boeing inertial upper stage (IUS), 21
bombers, 40

booster surveillance & tracking system (BSTS), 54
boost phase defence, 58-65, 90-1
Boyce, Christopher John, 13-14
Braun, Wernher von, 12

C
carbon fabrics, 31
Carter, Aston B., 68, 86
Carter, Jimmy, 13
'Cat House', 45
Central Intelligence Agency (CIA), 11, 13, 14, 15, 69
chaff, 92
Chair Heritage, 76
Challenger, 16
chemical lasers, 49, 65, 70-1
Chervov, Nikolai, 87
Cheyenne Mountain, Colorado, 8, 11, 23
China, satellites, 28
Clarke, Arthur C., 25, 93, 97
'Coda', 9
collisions in space, 18
computers, battle management, 82-3, 85-5
Consolidated Space Operations Center (CSOC), 11
Cooper, Robert, 31, 71, 84
Cosmos 4, 13
Cosmos 954, 18-19
Cosmos 1267, 30
Cosmos 1375, 27
Cosmos 1379, 27
counter measures:
    outfoxing the defence, 90-2
    overwhelming the defence, 92-7
    underlying the defence, 92
counter measures to SDI, 87-97
cruise missiles, 92

D
'Dauphin', 7
debris in orbit, 18-19
decoys, 83, 91-2
Defense Advanced Research Projects Agency (DARPA), 31, 70-1
Defense Intelligence Agency, 79
Defensive Technologies Study Team (DTST), 47-50, 64, 71
Delauer, Richard D., 91
Department of Defense (DOD), 13, 19, 20-21, 29, 30
designating optical tracker (DOT), 54
digital signal transmission, 15, 18
directed energy weapons, 53
Discoverer 13, 12

Discovery, 62-3
'Dog House', 45
Dombey, Norman, 73
Dyna-Soar, 12

E
early warning satellites, 13, 27
Edwards Air Force Base, 28
Eisenhower, Dwight D., 12, 39
electro-magnetic pulses (EMP), 25, 30, 31, 46
electromagnetic rail guns, 76-7, 79-82
electronic intelligence (ELINT), 14, 15, 16
electronic jamming, 31
electronic sensors, 15
electronic spy satellite, 16
electronic warfare weapons (EW), 31
ERIS, 78
Excalibur, 7
excimer lasers, 71-2
Explorer 1, 12

F
F-15 Eagle, 23, 28, 29, 30, 78
F-16 Falcon, 52
Fair, Harry, 80
Federal Bureau of Investigation (FBI), 13, 14
Federation of American Scientists, 35-6
'Ferret', 14, 15
fighting mirrors, 62-63
film return satellites, 18
Fiscal 1984–1988 Defense Guidance, 23
Fletcher, James C., 47-50, 64, 71
Fort Meade, 14
Fractional Orbit Bombardment System (FOBS), 26-7
Future Security Strategy Study (FSSS), 47, 49

G
Galosh, 45-6, 47
Garwin, Richard L., 27-8, 83, 90
General Electric Co., 55
geostationary orbit, 14, 20, 21
Gilpatric, Roswell, 26
Goddard Space Flight Center, 19
Gorbochev, Mikhail, 29, 30, 88
Gottfried, Kurt, 27-8
Graham, Daniel O., 8-9
Grand Forks Air Force Base, 26, 45
graphite coatings, 31
Grenada, 9
ground resolution, 15
Gromyko, Andrei, 36

Grumman Aerospace, 55

H
Hafner, Donald L., 27-8
Haig, Alexander, 6-7
Heiberg. Elvin R. II, 77
Heritage Foundation, 8
high altitude endo-atmospheric
    defense system (HEDS), 54
High Frontier Incorporated, 8
High Precision Tracking Experiment,
    63
Hoeber, Amoretta, 78
Hoffman, Fred C., 47, 49, 50
Homing Overlay Experiment (HOE),
    67, 77-8
Honeywell Inc., 55
Hoover Institution on War
    Revolution and Peace, 8
Howe, Sir Geoffrey, 38, 51
Hughes, John, 9
Hughes Aerospace, 54
hydrogen bombs, delivery, 40

I
ibn Salman ibn Abdulaziz, Sultan, 63
Iklé, Fred, 86
industry, SDI contracts, 53, 54-5
Inertial Upper Stage (IUS), 21
inter-continental ballistic missiles
    (ICBMs): 7, 14, 27, 28
    interception, 39-55, 57-69
    weapons against, 69-82
    counter-defence of, 87-97
intermediate range ballistic missiles
    (IRBMs), 27
Itek Optical, 55

J
Jane's Spaceflight Directory, 15
Jasani, Bhupendra, 10, 16, 18
Johnson, Lyndon B., 40-1
Johnston Island, 25-6, 46
Jupiter C., 12

K
Kamchatka, 16
Kampiles, William P., 14
Kapustin Yar missile site, 21
Kennedy, Edward, 7, 9
Kennedy, John F., 9, 16, 26, 40, 41, 95
KEW, 78
Key-Hole 8 (KH-8), 15, 16
Key-Hole 9 (KH-9), 15, 16
Key-Hole 11 (KH-11), 14-15, 18
Keyworth, George A., 7, 9, 12, 34,
    56, 58
KGB, 14
kinetic energy weapons, 53, 65, 67,
    76-9, 88
Kolm, Henry, 80
Korean Airline incident, 15-16
Krasnoyarsk radar station, 46
Kremlin, 36

Kwajalein Atoll, 39

L
laser weapons, 9, 29, 31-4, 57, 69-75
    chemical, 65, 70-1
    excimer, 71-2
    ground based, 62-4
    orbiting, 59-62
    X-ray, 64, 65, 72-5
Lawrence Livermore Laboratory,
    7, 57, 73, 75, 76, 87
Leasat F3, 21
Leasat, F4, 21
Lee, Andrew Daulton, 14
Lockheed Missiles & Space Co., 54
LODE, 70
LTV Corporation, 54
Lucid, Shannon, 63
Lyaki radar station, 46

M
McChord Air Force Base, 23
McCrery, James, 88
McDonnel Douglas Astronautics,
    53, 54
McFarlane, Robert 'Bud', 9
McNab, Ian, 77
McNamara, Robert S., 26
Martin Marietta Aerospace, 53, 55
Meyer, Stephen M., 95
mid-course defence, 65-8
Miniature Homing Intercept
    Vehicle (MHIV), 23, 28
MIRACL, 70
mirrors, 62-3, 72, 88
Mishelevka radar station, 46
missile gap, 40-1
Morning Light, operation, 19
Multiple Independently Targeted
    Re-entry Vehicles (MIRVs),
    41-3, 58, 65-6, 89
Multiple Re-entry Vehicles (MRVs)
Mutual Assured Destruction
    (MAD), 8, 9, 13, 49, 57
Mutual Assured Survival (MAS),
    49, 57
MX missiles, 9, 42, 64, 89

N
NASA, 12, 20, 51
National Council of the Federation
    of American Scientists, 35
National Security Agency, 13
National Space Strategy, 96
NATO, 18, 51
Nike-Zeus, 39, 44
Nitze, Paul H., 89
Nixon, Richard, 44
North American Defense Command
    (NORAD), 8, 11, 19, 84
Nuckolls, Harry, 81
nuclear explosions, space based,
    25-6
nuclear radiation, screening

against, 31
nuclear warheads, numbers, 42,
    43-4, 92-3
nuclear winter, 50
Nuclear x-ray laser, 7, 49, 64, 65, 72-5

O
Oakhanger, England, 11
O Group, 57
Olenegorsk radar station, 46
Operations Center, 14
Orr, Verne, 88

P
Parnas, David, 85
particle beam weapons, 9, 30, 49,
    65, 75-6, 88
Patriot, 47
Pechora radar station, 46
penetration aids, 66
Pentagon, 6-8, 12, 13, 21, 27, 30,
    34, 40, 46, 47, 53, 73
Perez de Cuellar, Javier, 96
Perle, Richard N., 35
Pershing II, 43
phased array radar stations, 46
Pike, John, 63
Plesetsk, 27
post-boost phase defence, 68
Pravda, 16
Program 437, 25-6
Puskino radar station, 46

R
'Rachel', 57
radioactive debris, 19
Rather, Dr, 71
RCA Government Systems
    Division, 53, 55
Re-entry Vehicle (RVs), 78, 89
Reagan, Ronald, 6-9, 20, 29, 36, 47,
    50, 53, 72, 74-5, 85, 94, 96
'Rhyolite', 14, 15
Rocketdyne, 71
Rockwell International
    Corporation, 55, 57
Rostow, Eugene, 44
Royal United Services Institute, 51

S
SA-10, 47
SA-X-12, 47
Safeguard, 44-5, 58
Sagan, Carl, 83
Sagdeyev, R. Z., 94
SAINT, 24-5
Salyut, 6, 30
Salyut 7, 21
SAM, 47
Sary Shagen, 29, 46
Satellite Control Facility, 11
satellite interceptor (SAINT), 24, 25
satellites:
    autonomy, 31

laser battle stations, 59-62
survivability, 31
Satellite Test Center, 11
Satellite Trading Unit, Canada, 11
Satka, 78
Schlesinger, James, 92, 97
Scientific American, 27
Sea Lite, 70
secret graphite coating, 31
Sentinel, 44
Sentry, 58
'seven hour nuclear war', 27
SH-4 rocket, 47
Shultz, George, 36
Skylight, 70
Space Command, 21, 53
space cruiser, 97
Space Defense Operations Center,
    6, 11, 23, 35
Space Detection and Tracking
    System (SPADATS), 11
Space Launch Complex Number 6, 20
space mines, 31, 35, 93
space shuttles, 16, 20-1, 51
space stations, manned, 21
'Spacetracks', 11
Space Transportation System, 21
Spartan, 44
Sprint, 44
Sputnik 1, 12
spy satellites, 11-21
Squanto Terror, 25-6
SS-9 intercontinental ballistic missile,
    26-27, 35
SS-20 missile, 27, 43
Star Wars *see* Strategic Defense
    Initiative
State Department, 7, 40
Stevens, Senator, 9
Stockholm International Peace
    Research Institute (SIPRI): 16, 18
Strategic Air Command, 84
Strategic Arms Limitation Talks
    (SALT 1), 42
Strategic Arms Limitation Treaty
    (SALT II), 27
strategic communications satellite
    system, 28
Strategic Defense Initiative (SDI),
    7, 9, 24, 30, 36, 37, 44, 47, 50-5
    basing, 59
    battle management, 82-5
    boost phase defence, 58-65, 90-1
    component parts of, 21
    contracts, 53, 54-5
    counter measures, 87-97
    ground based laser weapons, 62-4
    mid-course defence, 65-8
    orbiting laser battle stations, 59-62
    pop-up system, 64-5
    post-boost phase defence, 65
    Reagan announces, 6-9
    terminal phase defence, 68-9
    weapons, 69-82

Strategic Defense Initiative
    Organization (SDIO), 50
Strategic Defense System, 20
STS-8 Challenger, 16
SU-15 interceptor, 16
submarine-launched ballistic
    missiles (SLBMs), 27, 42, 47, 92
Sunnyvale, 11
System Generated
    Electromagnetic Pulse, 30

T
Talon Gold, 70
Teal Ruby, 84
Teldyne Brown Engineering Inc., 54
Teller, Edward, 7, 8, 27, 57, 71, 72, 75
terminal phase defence, 68-9
Test Ban Treaty, 26
Thompson, Henry, 82
Thor-Agena rocket, 13
Thor missile, 25, 26
Thule, Greenland, 11
Time magazine, 29
Titan, 34D, 15
The Times, 7, 50
tracking and surveillance systems, 53
Triad, 70
Trident, 53
TRW, 11, 13, 55, 71
Try Add radar, 45
Tsipsis, Kosta, 96
Tyuratum, 13, 26-7

U
U-2 spy plane, 13
Union of Concerned Scientists, 83
US Army, 12
US Navy, 70
    Space Surveillance System, 11
USAF, 12, 16, 18, 20, 23-6, 70, 80
    Satellite Control Facility, 19
    Space Command, 11, 31, 51
US remote tracking stations, 11

V
Validator, 83-4
Vandenberg Air Force Base, 11, 13,
    16, 21

W
Washington DC, 6, 8
Weinberger, Caspar, 6, 48, 50, 69,
    88, 95-5
We Must Defend America, 8
Westinghouse Electronics
    Corporation, 55
White House, 6, 9, 23, 27, 40, 53, 57
Wood, Lowell, 57

X
X-rays lasers, 7, 49, 64, 65, 72-5

Z
Zavali, Michael, 14

PICTURE CREDITS
Associated Press: 13
Military Archive Research Ser-vices: Title page, endpapers, contents, 6,
7 Dept of Defense, 8/9 Martin Marietta,
10, 11, 12, 14, 15, 19, 20, 21 Dept of
Defense, 22 Dept of Defense, 24/5 US Air
Force, 27, 28, 29, 31, 35 Dept of Defense,
36 Dept of Defense, 36/7, 38 US Army, 39
US Army, 40(tl) US Army, 40(tr) US Navy,
40(br) US Navy, 41 Martin Marietta Aero-
space, 42 US Navy, 43 Dept of Defense,
44, 44/5, 45, 46 Dept of Defense, 47 Dept
of Defense, 49 Martin Marietta Aero-
space, 50, 50/1, 52 Martin Marietta
Aerospace, 52/3 US Air Force, 53, 56
NASA, 59 Dept of Defense, 62, 63 Dept of
Defense, 66/7 US Air Force/Salamander,
67 Dept of Defense, 68 US Navy, 69, 70/1
US Air Force, 71, 73 US Air Force, 75 US
Air Force, 76 Dept of Defense, 77 Dept of
Defense, 80 Dept of Defense, 82, 83 US
Air Force, 84 US Air Force, 85, 86, 87 Dept
of Defense, 88/9, 89, 90/1 DofD, 92, 93,
94, 95, 96, 97, 100/1.
Novosti Press Agency (APN): 88
Science Photo Library: 74/5 Alexan-
der Tsiaras
US Air Force: 34, 48

ARTWORK
Simon Roulstone: 16, 17, 30/1, 32/3, 60/1,
64/5, 72
Ian Stephen: 18/9

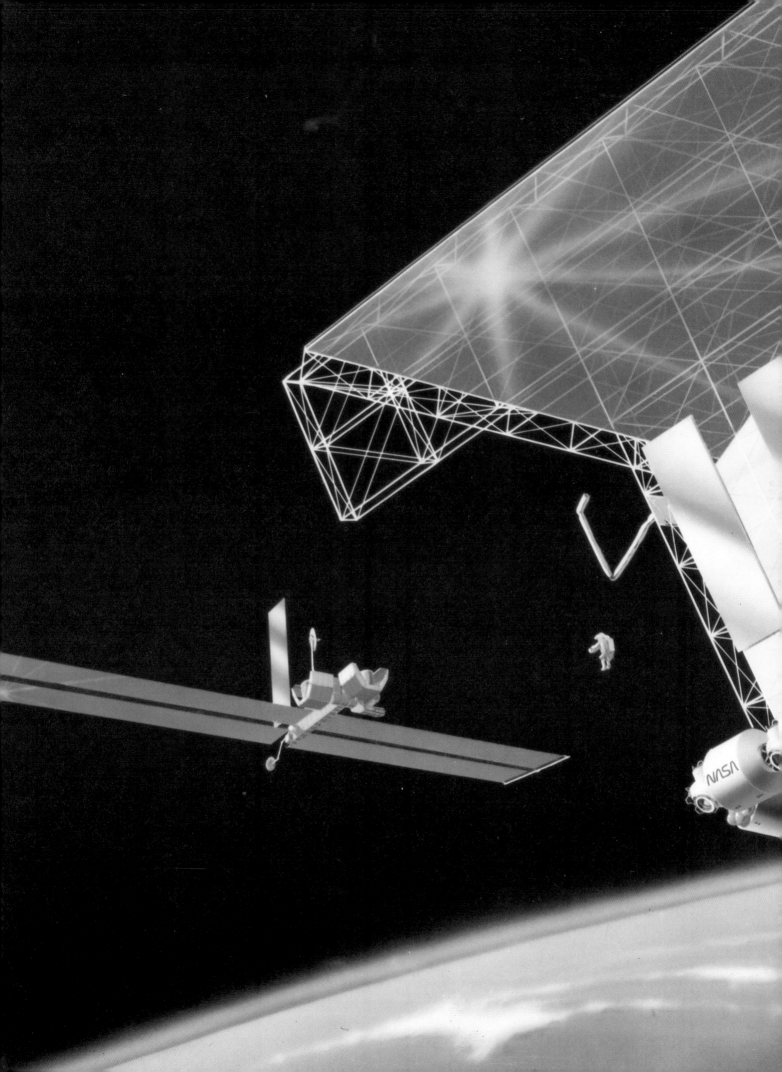